brains on! PRESENTS...

ROAD TRIP EARTH

brains on! ®

PRESENTS...

ROAD TRIP EARTH

EXPLORE OUR AWESOME PLANET, FROM CORE TO SHORE AND SO MUCH MORE

MOLLY BLOOM, MARC SANCHEZ, AND SANDEN TOTTEN

WITH MEGAN E. BRYANT

Little, Brown and Company

New York Boston

This book is for all the curious kids and brilliant scientists who power *Brains On!*, and give us hope for the future of this planet.

About This Book

The illustrations for this book were rendered digitally. This book was edited by Samantha Gentry and designed by Neil Swaab. The production was supervised by Bernadette Flinn, and the production editor was Jen Graham. The text was set in Bembo Std, and the display type is KG Second Chances and KG Tangled Up In You 2.

Little, Brown and Company
Hachette Book Group
1290 Avenue of the Americas, New York, NY 10104
Visit us at LBYR.com

First Edition: March 2022

Little, Brown and Company is a division of Hachette Book Group, Inc.
The Little, Brown name and logo are trademarks of Hachette Book Group, Inc.

The publisher is not responsible for websites (or their content) that are not owned by the publisher.

Library of Congress Cataloging-in-Publication Data
Names: Bloom, Molly, 1983– author.
Title: Brains on! presents…road trip earth : explore our awesome planet, from core to shore and so much more / Molly Bloom, Marc Sanchez, and Sanden Totten.
Description: First edition. | New York : Little, Brown and Company, 2022. | Includes bibliographical references and index. | Audience: Ages 8–12 | Summary: "The creators of *Brains On!*, the award-winning science podcast for kids, take readers on a journey through Earth—from the core to the outer atmosphere, and everywhere in between." —Provided by publisher.
Identifiers: LCCN 2021016147 | ISBN 9780316459365 | ISBN 9780316459396 (ebook)
Subjects: LCSH: Earth (Planet)—Juvenile literature.
Classification: LCC QB631.4 .B594 2022 | DDC 525—dc23
LC record available at https://lccn.loc.gov/2021016147

ISBNs: 978-0-316-45936-5 (hardcover), 978-0-316-45939-6 (ebook), 978-0-316-45938-9 (ebook), 978-0-316-45937-2 (ebook)

PRINTED IN CHINA

1010

10 9 8 7 6 5 4 3 2 1

Contents

Introduction

We're the hosts of the podcast *Brains On!* You probably already know we're serious about being curious—which means we love to answer important questions like:

We've got so many questions, and we want some answers! So we're embarking on an epic road trip to uncover the coolest facts, strangest mysteries, and most incredible marvels of planet Earth.

We're going to dig deep and discover what's hidden underground—and find out about our planet's past. We'll explore the watery mysteries of the oceans and the mind-blowing properties of water itself. We'll roam the surface of the earth and get dirty, muddy, sandy, sweaty, frosty, and wet in the process. And last—but definitely not least—we're going to blast off to experience the sky-high wonders of our atmosphere.

Best of all, we have room for you to come along!

Enter the ExPLORERR!

How will we travel from the deepest depths of the earth to the highest heights of the atmosphere? Well, we could take a variety of vehicles, from a submarine to a rocket… or we could test-drive a new ride we cooked up at *Brains On!* Headquarters, the ExPLORERR (which stands for **Ex**tremely **P**ractical **L**and & **O**cean **R**over **E**xploring **R**emote **R**ealms)!

Yes, we know it looks like a minivan. We think that's part of the charm. And even though it could definitely get you safely to soccer practice, dance class, and summer camp, this is not your average minivan. This one-of-a-kind machine can adapt to survive in any environment. Think about it: The ExPLORERR will have to handle extreme temperatures, extreme pressure, and extreme elevation. Is it up to the job?

We're about to find out.

We've got state-of-the-art navigation equipment as well as good old-fashioned maps and compasses. We've got superthick glass panels, spiked wheels that double as flotation devices, and some heavy-duty windshield wipers that can tackle rain, snow, lava, and all the dead bugs that go *splat* on the windshield. *And* the ExPLORERR even has a little kitchen! After all, a trip this epic demands some awesome snacks.

So buckle your seat belt and get ready for an incredible road (and off-road!) trip.

PART I
INTO THE EARTH

THIS CORE IS NO BORE

We've mapped out our route. We've got our road-trip party playlist ready to go. Anyone need to hit the restroom before we leave? You sure? Okay. Let's rock! Or more specifically, let's *dig* through rock. Because we're going to burrow way down deep—all the way to the core—and check out the earth's guts!

> But first things first, we need some supplies. It's going to be super hot and super dark down at the center of the earth. Plus, we'll have the entire weight of the world pushing on us from every side. I hope you're good under pressure!

PACKING LIST

- ☑ Flashlights and headlamps (for darkness!)
- ☑ Fans and ice packs (for hotness!)
- ☑ Helmets (for brain protection!)
- ☑ Pressure-proof suits (stylish and functional!)
- ☑ Crossword puzzles (for keeping our neurons nimble!)
- ☑ Oven mitts

> Just in case! After all, it's like a mega-oven down there!

And in addition to supplies, let's make sure all snacks are present and accounted for.

SNACKING LIST

Since we'll be tunneling through the layers of the earth, we've got some layered goodies to munch on!

- ☑ Layer cake
- ☑ Lasagna
- ☑ Seven-layer dip (with extra chips, of course!)
- ☑ Lava cake (Note: Make sure it's *chocolate* lava and not *actual* lava!)
- ☑ Stuffed-crust pizza (emphasis on the crust!)
- ☑ And of course, the ultimate layered food...build-your-own sandwiches!

EXPLORERR MAKEOVERR

- ✔ An incredibly strong, capsule-shaped shell helps the ExPLORERR withstand the massive pressure found deep underground.

- ✔ The Thermoshield keeps us cool even when the temperature in the earth's core hits more than 10,000 degrees Fahrenheit (now, that's hotter than sunbathing with a fire-breathing dragon!).

- ✔ A row of spotlights to help brighten up even the darkest places.

- ✔ A sharp, diamond-tipped drill that can tunnel all the way to the center of the earth.

WARNING! Our journey to the center of the earth will be fraught with dangers, like intense pressure and heat. But scariest of all—there are no bathrooms down there! So go now or forever hold your pees.

3

Looks like we're ready to roll. To get to the center of the earth, we're going to drill about 4,000 miles underground. While we're doing that, let's learn about the history of this planet we're currently putting a giant hole in.

It all started about 14 billion—yes, that's *billion* with a B—years ago. That's the moment when the universe popped into existence. Of course, none of us were around back then to see it. But scientists have come up with a really cool idea to explain it: the big bang theory. Scientists think that back then everything that would come to be in the universe was smushed into a tiny dot, which suddenly exploded. That's where the big bang name comes from. When this explosion happened, it scattered lots of material—most of which was hydrogen. This hydrogen combined with helium to form stars.

Think of the baby universe like a bowl of cosmic soup, filled with all kinds of tasty morsels just floating around in space. Gases and dust bits and noodles. Wait, no, noodles are for regular soup, not cosmic soup. Anyway, a force called gravity began to slowly pull little islands of material together, forming the first galaxies. Now, instead of space soup, we've got a buffet of cosmic snacks, like stars and galaxies, including our own galaxy—the Milky

Way. But still no plan-
ets. For those to enter
the picture, we need
some stars to explode.

Stars are like giant
space ovens. As they
burn, they cook up super
important elements, like
carbon, oxygen, and
even gold. These things
weren't around right after
the big bang, but stars
made lots of them over
time. When these stars
died, they exploded and

released all those super useful materials out into the universe. It's those materials that eventually became the raw ingredients for planets like ours. If you fast-forward about 10 billion years, our very own planet started to form, thanks to one very special star—our sun.

Our sun was born from a big old cloud of gas and dust. As gravity pulled the cloud together, it got denser and denser until it became a star. While the sun was forming, it was spinning, which caused a disk of gas to collect around it. Gas and dust and ice started to clump together, making planetesimals (or itty-bitty planets). These planetesimals started smashing into one another like deep-space bumper cars, forming bigger chunks that smashed into even *bigger* chunks. The next thing you know, actual planets started to form!

BREAK IT DOWN
PLANETESIMAL

Planet- = planet

-esimal = very tiny (from infinitesimal)

Aww. Baby Earth is so adorable.

Does that mean kittens should be called liontesimals? And Ping-Pong should be tennistesimal?

Big planets like Saturn and Jupiter formed first. They were already giants before Earth started to form. Then something happened that changed our solar system forever.

When the sun finished forming, it suddenly turned on like a giant furnace. It began to make sunlight and let out a huge gust of solar wind. *WHOOSH!* The wind blew lighter elements farther out into the solar system, but it left behind the heavier material that created Earth.

ANATOMY OF EARTH

Whew! We made it to the center of the earth—and yes, it is hotter than an oven filled with ghost peppers down here. When the planet formed approximately 4.5 billion years ago, it developed a super hot center that's still cooling off—kind of like a freshly baked cookie that's still warm in the middle. Here are the layers that make up our most excellent home:

- **The core** has two layers—the inner core and the outer core.

- **The mantle** is the biggest layer inside the earth.

- **The crust** is the thinnest layer of all the earth's layers—and the one where we live.

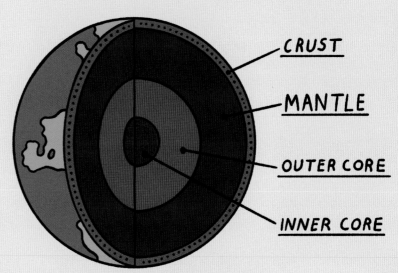

CRUST

MANTLE

OUTER CORE

INNER CORE

Encore (More About the Core)

The dense inner core is basically a 1,500-mile-wide massive pinball of solid metal. It's mostly made of iron, and it's constantly rotating.

The outer core is like a warm, toasty blanket that covers the inner core. A very warm, very toasty blanket that is as hot as the surface

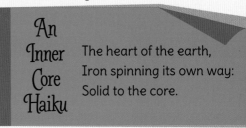

An Inner Core Haiku

The heart of the earth,
Iron spinning its own way:
Solid to the core.

An Outer Core Haiku

Swirl, whirl, swish, swoosh, *whoosh!*
Melted metal churns and burns.
Look, but do *not* touch!

Haiku are three-line poems of Japanese origin, where the first line has five syllables, the second has seven, and the third has five. Like:

Sanden, Molly, Marc
Are most serious about
Being curious.

of the sun and would melt pretty much anything it touched. Plus, this outer core is made of molten liquid *and* it creates the earth's magnetic field. We'll talk more about this later, but just know that because of this magnetic field, we have an atmosphere that makes it possible for all life on this planet to exist. Since we like existing, we're big fans of the outer core and its magnetic field.

Meet the Mantle

If the core is like the gooey center of a cookie, the next layer is like the harder, chewier part that surrounds that center. It's called the mantle, and it is the thickest of the earth's four layers. There's still a lot for us to learn about this middle section. In fact, scientists suspect that the mantle is more layered and varied than we know, with super secret, hidden layers. The mantle likes to keep things mysterious.

A Mantle Haiku

The big mystery,
Mantle, is why your secrets
Are buried so deep.

One cool fact about the mantle is that it's where diamonds form. Since most people don't have an ExPLORERR at their disposal, they can't just travel down here to get them. Lucky for bling lovers everywhere, a long time ago, underground eruptions pushed some diamonds up closer to the planet's surface. That's how we are able to find them today.

A Crust Haiku

We walk over you,
Never stopping to say, hey—
Thanks for being there!

Crust for Us!

Quick, name your favorite crust! Pie crust? Pizza crust? Bread crust? For us, it has to be the earth's crust. Sure, it's not as delicious, but it's much easier to live on. After all, the crust covers the entire surface of the planet, from the ocean floor to mountains and deserts. That doesn't mean that the crust is the same everywhere, though. Some parts are thicker, some parts are thinner, and some parts are still growing right now!

HEAVY METAL AND THE MAGNETIC FIELD

The earth is covered by an amazing, invisible magnetic field. This incredible shield around our planet has made it possible for all life to exist here. Think of it like a bubble that traps the air in our atmosphere so it doesn't float off into space. It also blocks harmful cosmic rays from frying us little earthlings. But where does the magnetic field come from?

The core!

PIT STOP

THE KOLA SUPERDEEP BOREHOLE

Let's take a quick detour to the deepest hole ever dug: the Kola Superdeep Borehole! Scientists from Russia started digging this hole in 1970, north of the Arctic Circle. For more than twenty years, a crew kept digging deeper...and deeper...and deeper...until at last, in 1992, the Kola Superdeep Borehole reached its deepest depth: 40,230 feet, to be precise.

So why did they stop? One word: heat. When they came in contact with temperatures greater than 350 degrees Fahrenheit, drilling at Kola came to an end. Heat like that can quickly damage even the strongest equipment, and it causes other problems too. As the temperature rises, the land becomes more liquid, which can make drilling next to impossible.

Scientists may have abandoned the Kola Superdeep Borehole, but they definitely haven't given up on their quest to reach the mantle. If we could study the mantle up close, we could learn so much more about volcanoes, earthquakes, and how the mantle affects our planet and our lives.

The liquid molten metal of the outer core is constantly moving, swirling around like the whooshy insides of a lava lamp. Hot metal rises from the bottom of the core. When it reaches the top of the core, it cools down and begins to sink back to the bottom. Then it gets heated again—and rises again—and you get the picture. It's a dancing, churning, spinning mosh pit of molten goo. Now, *that's* heavy metal (air guitar!). The constant motion of the metal is what generates the earth's magnetic field. Nice work, outer core!

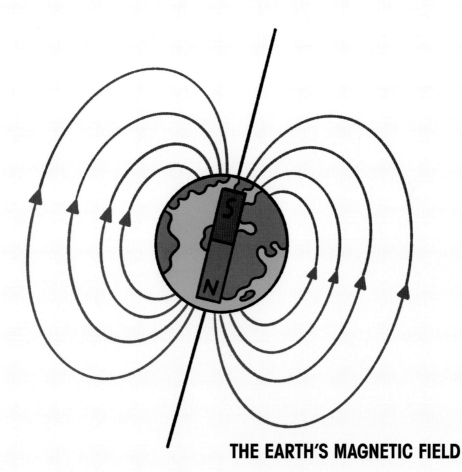

THE EARTH'S MAGNETIC FIELD

ON THE EARTH'S PLATES

We humans have spent our entire existence on the earth's crust, so you'd think we'd know it pretty well. But it wasn't that long ago that we found out it's not actually one solid chunk covering the whole planet. It's actually made up of several broken pieces that float on top of the mantle. We call these pieces tectonic plates.

WHEN CONTINENTS COLLIDE!

Your dinner plates can be pretty big—especially on Thanksgiving—but they're nothing compared to tectonic plates. Tectonic plates are massive slabs of rock that cover the whole planet, which means they are even underwater too. Tectonic plates are constantly moving, ever so slowly, sliding atop the gooey, squelchy mantle. They move so slowly that most of the time, we don't notice. In fact, tectonic plates move only about an

FACT-ASTIC VOYAGE

The word "tectonic" is based on the Greek word for building. Tectonic plates essentially *build* the landscape around us.

It's a tie!

inch a year—which is, coincidentally, about how much your fingernails grow in a year too. When your fingernails move, they can scratch itches or pick scabs. When tectonic plates move, they can reshape the entire planet! Think mountains… earthquakes…and volcanoes!

Mountains: Tip-Top Earth

When a tectonic plate moves around on the mantle, sometimes it will collide with another tectonic plate. When these massive slabs push into each other, they create giant mounds of earth. The result? Mountains!

- **Fold mountain:** Two tectonic plates collide, forming one of the tallest mountain structures on the planet.

- **Plateau mountain:** Two plates bump but don't buckle or fold; plateau mountains do not have the traditional pointy-peaked mountain shape.

- **Volcanic mountain:** These mountains start as little cracks in the ground, where hot material shoots out and collects around the crack, eventually forming a mountain!

The tallest mountain on earth is Mount Everest. It's over 29,000 feet tall! It's truly the upper crust.

Earthquakes: Moving and Shaking

Choose the right answer: Earthquakes are caused by (A) a group of more than fifty people jumping at the exact same time; (B) Thor's Hammer slipping out of its, uh, hammer holder; (C) tectonic plates.

If you guessed C, congratulations. But seriously, don't get on Thor's bad side. That hammer is MIGHTY!

Tectonic plates have rough, jagged edges. These edges often slide up and push against the sides of other plates. We call the spot where they meet a fault. As these plates slide against each other, they can get stuck, which creates tension along the fault. Pressure from this tension builds up until it has enough power to knock the plates loose again—causing an earthquake! When this happens, powerful shock waves flow through the plates like ripples through a pond.

Some, but not all, earthquakes will have foreshocks. Those are like mini earthquakes that happen before the big earthquake, which is called the mainshock. All earthquakes have aftershocks, which are smaller quakes that follow the mainshock. Just because they are smaller doesn't mean they're harmless. Aftershocks can cause plenty of damage too.

I blame tectonic plates for quakes. It's always their *fault*!

CAN ANIMALS PREDICT EARTHQUAKES?

For thousands of years, people have wondered if animals can sense that an earthquake is coming before it hits. Well, the answer is a definite...we don't know! People have been observing strange animal behavior before quakes since 373 BCE—more than 2,000 years ago. For example, in China in 1975, hibernating snakes suddenly awoke and slithered away before serious shaking started. Once, just before an earthquake in Italy in 1976, people noticed mice scurrying around and farm animals acting restless.

However, it's not consistent. Sometimes big earthquakes happen without animals acting weird first. Scientists are still studying this phenomenon to see if it's real, and if it is, how it works. If animals could give us a heads-up when a powerful quake is about to hit, it could save lives.

Volcanoes: Lava on Tap

There are a lot of amazing things under our feet, like colonies of ants, ancient fossils, and—if this old map we found is correct—buried pirates' treasure. But perhaps the most amazing thing of all is…*magma*! *Magma* is the word for super hot, melted, gooey, liquid rocks. And far below the crust, there is a lot of it. Which is where we like it, because magma is like a person with bad breath—best to keep your distance. But sometimes it comes to the surface, thanks to volcanoes.

Volcanoes, like earthquakes, are made by tectonic plates. One way they form is when two plates meet and one plate gets pushed under the other. Some of the molten-hot magma, or melted rocks, beneath the crust then finds a way to burst up and out, creating a volcano! This is also how volcanic mountains are formed.

Hot spots are places in the mantle where heat from deep within the earth warms up rocky material, causing it to rise. As it rises, it gets hotter and hotter and starts to feel less pressure. The result is magma.

Where the mantle meets the lower part of the crust, the magma begins to form large clumps. These red-hot liquid rocks keep rising in a magma chamber—a place where magma gathers far below the surface of the earth. As more and more magma fills the chamber, the magma gets closer and closer to the earth's surface. Then gas starts bubbling out of the magma—*blurp blurp*. The pressure increases and cracks the surrounding rocks. Uh-oh.

When the pressure gets high enough, look out! The magma will explode through the earth's surface in an eruption! Think of it like a fiery-hot earth burp. If that happens again and again in the same place, it creates a volcano.

You're going to *lava* this next part. Once the magma bursts out of the crust, it has a new name: lava. It's still super dangerous, though, so stand back!

Sometimes, magma bubbles up to the earth's surface but *doesn't* explode through the crust. What happens then? It's the birth of a new landform called a dome mountain. You could think of dome mountains as earth sculptures. The magma pushes the crust upward, and forces of nature like wind and rain do the rest to shape these majestic mounds.

HOT MAGMA, COOL ISLANDS

Aloha! It's me, Hawaii, also known as the Big Island.

I bet you're wondering how I got all the way out here in the middle of the water.

Well, let me tell you! The Hawaiian Islands are located over a hot spot in the Pacific Ocean.

HOT SPOT

As a tectonic plate moves over the hot spot, molten magma burbles up to form a volcano.

The plate keeps slowly moving and eventually forms another volcano.

BLURP!

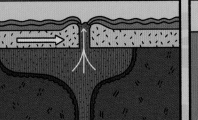

Every Hawaiian island is made up of at least one volcano. And I'm made of five different volcanoes! No wonder they call me the Big Island!

The hot spot doesn't move, but the plate does—it keeps sliding forward, and over millions of years, those volcanoes formed the Hawaiian Archipelago, a group of more than 130 islands.

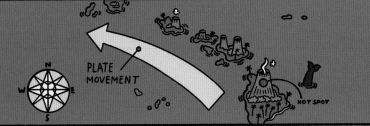

PLATE MOVEMENT

N
W E
S

HOT SPOT

I hope you visit sometime! I might be near a hot spot, but I like to think I'm a pretty cool island. Aloha!

Archipelago: an area of water that contains several scattered islands

SUPER COOL SCIENTIST

DR. CAROLYN PARCHETA

Dr. Carolyn Parcheta is a volcanologist—an expert in volcanoes. Carolyn and her team created a special robot named VolcanoBot to explore the insides of volcanoes! It's about the size of a loaf of bread, with a wheel on both ends and a camera in the middle. The two wheels are covered with spikes so it can grip surfaces and even climb up walls! One of VolcanoBot's most important missions so far sent it into a fissure, or crack in the earth, that appeared on Kilauea (Kill-uh-WAY-uh), a volcano in Hawaii. A fissure erupts magma, and it's the most common style of eruption on earth. After an eruption happens, though, the fissure usually gets clogged with magma, and scientists can no longer access it.

For some reason, the fissure on Kilauea didn't get clogged, so VolcanoBot explored it to find out more. It gathered data that helped Carolyn and her team create a 3-D map of the fissure. VolcanoBot's journey was so successful that Carolyn was inspired to create Volcano-Bot 2. The new version has a stronger motor, is more lightweight, and collects more data. Carolyn hopes it will help us understand how eruptions happen—which will help us better understand our planet.

HOT COLORS

The color of lava changes depending on its temperature.

YELLOW	ORANGE	RED	BLACK
Still incredibly, blisteringly hot.	Cooling down.	Even cooler (but trust us, you still don't want to touch it).	Coolest; the lava has transitioned from liquid to solid and is turning into glass.

MEGA MATCHUP
LAVA VS. DIAMONDS

Now it's time for a face-off between two mysterious marvels from the mantle. In one corner, lava! It's hot, it's unstoppable, and it's creating new landmasses as we speak. And in the other corner, diamonds! Not just a sparkly stone, diamonds are tough—one of the hardest substances we've ever discovered.

TEAM LAVA

- Lethal lava is basically burning rock that's so hot it has melted. If you thought solid rocks were tough, just wait till you see them in liquid form.

- Most lava is so hot that it glows. We're talking temperatures of 2,000 degrees Fahrenheit and hotter. That's ten times as hot as boiling water!

- Lava is the ultimate destroyer. If you drop your favorite pocketknife, coin collection, or anvil into a lava flow, cherish your memories, because that thing is TOAST. Obliterated. Buh-byeee! It's forever lost to lava.

- Lava is the ultimate creator too. After it bursts out of a volcano, it cools to form new land! After lava burns through a forest, new plant growth reinvigorates the landscape.

- You can even find lava in space. For example, one of Jupiter's moons has a volcano that spews lava all day long. There's even a far-off planet that scientists think is entirely covered in lava!

TEAM DIAMOND

- Diamonds are one of the hardest natural substances in the world. They are so strong that the only thing that can cut a diamond is...another diamond!

- Diamonds are created in the mantle layer of the earth, where EXTREME heat and pressure combine forces to create something truly brilliant out of a single element: carbon.

- Diamonds in the wild don't glitter the way diamonds in jewelry do—instead, they have a dull gleam, almost like a piece of dirty ice. Diamonds must be cut to have many different facets, or sides, to show off their full sparkle.

- Diamonds aren't just for jewelry. Their strength and hardness make them important industrial tools for jobs like grinding, cutting, polishing, and drilling. Diamonds are even used in dentists' tools. Think about that the next time you see a sparkling smile.

- Meteors that have crashed into the earth have brought a big surprise with them: incredibly tiny diamonds! This proves they exist in space too.

Which earth-made marvel is cooler: Lava or Diamonds?

YOUR VERDICT

THE PANGAEA PUZZLE

Earth has several large landmasses, or continents, which are spread all around the globe. Since the tectonic plates are moving, the continents are too. If you look at a map of all the continents, you might start to notice that their edges almost seem like they could fit together like puzzle pieces. If you could slide the continents across the oceans until they joined, they would form one massive supercontinent.

Pangaea: the name of the ancient supercontinent

Could such a thing ever happen?

Scientists think it already did.

Evidence shows that long, long ago, all the continents made up one supercontinent. Eventually, they broke apart, and the movement of the plates helped them spread out around the globe. Plate tectonics, which helps explain this movement, is a fairly recent discovery and wasn't a widely accepted theory until the 1960s.

Hey! Where did the Atlantis piece go?

Huh. I guess we lost it.

BONE VOYAGE!

If tectonic plates are soooo big…and they move soooo slowly…then how do scientists know they move at all?

Just ask the bones!

There are striking similarities between fossils found on continents as far apart as Africa and South America. How on earth could prehistoric animals travel from one continent to another? We know they didn't have jets to fly them around. We also know they didn't use giant slingshots and parachutes to fling their bodies across the ocean. And we're pretty sure* they didn't go sailing from one continent to another on luxury yachts.

Consider this: If the continents were connected, the creatures could have been hanging out when the landmass split apart—leaving some animals on one side and some on the other. Scientists think that's how *Cynognathus* fossils ended up only in South America and Africa, even though these continents are an ocean apart. Fossils from *Lystrosaurus*, an ancient reptile, have been found in India, Antarctica, and South Africa, leading us to believe that these places were once connected.

---

*Make that definitely sure. We are *definitely* sure that they didn't have boats of any kind.

Road Trip
SOUVENIR

ZIRCON CRYSTALS

Zircon crystals are one of the coolest—and oldest—things on earth. Scientists have discovered a zircon crystal that is almost 4.4 billion years old, and because the earth itself is about 4.5 billion years old, these crystals have been around since almost the very beginning of our planet. That also means that zircon crystals have survived a lot, from earthquakes and meteor strikes to ice ages and duckface selfies! Zircon is a seriously strong mineral.

They also contain traces of other elements that were found on earth when the crystal first formed. By identifying these elements, scientists can get a better idea of what our planet was like in its earliest form—and even how life began. It's like a baby picture of earth hidden deep in this special rock.

MYSTERY PHOTO

Focus your eyes on this mystery photo. Can you guess what it is? Turn to the next page for the answer!

ANSWER!

It's one of the oldest fossils ever found—and it contains evidence of early life on earth! The first life-forms that we know of were microscopic, which means that they're invisible without using sophisticated tools to spot them in ancient rocks. There's a special name for these minuscule fossils: microfossils. Some microfossils are from life-forms that no longer exist, while others are closely related to microorganisms that are still present today—micro high five!

EXPLORERR MAKEOVERR

Time to get the ExPLORERR ready for our next destination: the deep sea! The good news is that we're halfway ready. The current modifications that helped us survive the extreme temperatures, extreme pressure, and extreme darkness under the earth will be needed underwater too.

KEEPING

✔ Capsule-shaped shell

✔ Thermoshield (soon it will protect us from *cold* temps)

✔ Row of spotlights

ADDING

✔ Waterproof layer

✔ Fins

✔ ScanSensor to find and repair any cracks or weak spots, especially in the windows

We Lava It Here!

Hi, Friend!

We made it to the center of the earth—and wow, do we have tales to tell! Between the heat and the pressure found under the earth's surface, it's safe to say that something exciting is always cooking down here. However, it is <u>not</u> safe to get too close. We've seen what 2,000-plus-degree magma can do, and it's not pretty. But it <u>is</u> pretty gooey.

When you think about it, it makes sense that a planet as unique and incredible as the earth would be filled with secrets and mysteries. The ones scientists have discovered so far make us hungry to learn more about our remarkable planet...and hungry to hit our snack stash too—earth core s'mores, anyone? Time for some nibbles while we travel to our next adventure—the deep sea!

Stay cool,
Molly, Marc, and Sanden

Brains On! BFF
Favorite Reading Spot
Earth, 3rd Planet from the Sun
Milky Way

PART 2
WET, WILD, AND WEIRD

UNDER WHERE? UNDERWATER!

Water's not just for drinking, swimming, bathing, cooking, shipping stuff across the ocean, being the home to thousands of species, and making it possible for life as we know it to exist. There's so much more! Are you ready to wind through the wondrous world of water and submerge yourself in the secrets of the sea? Great! But before we take the plunge, let's check our supplies.

WARNING! We're about to go deep, deep, deep underwater—where a force called hydrostatic pressure pose[s] a serious risk to people. Hydrostatic pressure is the weight you feel from water when you're su[r]rounded by it. The deeper you get, the more hydrostatic pressure pushes on you—and without t[he] right equipment, it can crush you! If you're like us, you'd rather avoid that.

Hold up! Before we journey into the ocean, let's double-check our packing list.

PACKING LIST

In the ExPLORERR, we have a perfectly controlled climate to protect us from the dangers of frigid temperatures and hydrostatic pressure. We won't be leaving the vehicle under any circumstances, so no need for scuba suits. But when you're going deep down below the surface, it never hurts to bring...

- ☑ Extra oxygen tanks
- ☑ Backup light sources (flashlights, lanterns, and headlamps)
- ☑ Radio communication with *Brains On!* Headquarters
- ☑ A little light reading like *20,000 Leagues Under the Sea*, *Moby-Dick*, and *The Old Man and the Sea*
- ☑ A bag of soil (in case you miss dry land)

SNACKING LIST

In honor of the salty ocean water, we're bringing our favorite salty snacks!

- ☑ Chips
- ☑ Seaweed
- ☑ Popcorn
- ☑ Pretzels
- ☑ Fish crackers
- ☑ Saltwater taffy

And don't forget about our snacking list!

All those savory snacks are bound to make us thirsty, so we can't forget drinks. Since the human body can be anywhere from 50 to nearly 80 percent water, it's important to stay hydrated. You may be surrounded by water in the ocean, but it's definitely not drinkable. In fact, drinking seawater can make you sick or even kill you. (For more info about the salt in ocean water, check out page 45.) So, to be on the safe side, we've filled up our water bottles and even brought a portable desalination machine just in case we need to make ocean water drinkable. Also, a de*saliva*tion machine might be in order in case we start drooling over these yummy snacks!

Desalination: the process of removing salt from water

Seeing the bottom of the ocean is on my bucket list! I can't wait!

Speaking of buckets, let's hope we don't spring a leak.

Don't worry! This vehicle is waterproof... I think. Here we go!

HOT TIMES AT THE HYDROTHERMAL VENTS

Bye-bye, earth's core. Hello, ocean floor!

Whoosh!

The ExPLORERR shoots out from a crack in the earth's crust on a column of smoky, steamy water.

Wheeee!

FACT-ASTIC VOYAGE

More than 70 percent of the world's volcanic activity happens underwater, where we never see it.

This would make an excellent theme park ride… if it weren't also super dangerous. That's because all around us, water is seeping into cracks in the earth and mixing with *magma*. That's right, we're surrounded by UNDERWATER VOLCANOES!

The magma heats the water and mixes it with some pretty serious—even dangerous—chemicals like hydrogen sulfide, methane, and hydrogen. Then— *spshewwww!*—that hot, smelly mess spurts back out of the ocean floor through one of the many cracks, known as hydrothermal vents. The result is a scorching, stinky stew that's even deadlier than the expired clam chowder growing mold in your fridge. But for deep-sea bacteria, this soup is life!

BREAK IT DOWN
HYDROTHERMAL VENT

Hydro- = water

-thermal = hot

vent = wind

MySTERy PHOTO

Focus your eyes on this mystery photo. Can you guess what it is? Turn to page 29 for the answer!

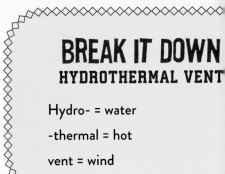

The Chemosynthesis Café

Good luck getting a dinner reservation on the ocean floor. There's no pizza place, no burger joint...not even a vending machine! So what do deep-sea dwellers eat? Well, in sunnier parts of the world, the food chain starts with plants. It works like this: Plants take energy from the sun, combine it with carbon dioxide from the air, and presto! They produce sugars and carbohydrates! This is called photosynthesis, and it's basically a plant superpower. Animals then eat the plants and get energy from those sugars and carbs. But here in the deep, dark depths of the ocean, there's no sun, no plants, and no photosynthesis.

So you'd think there'd be no food, but it turns out there's another way to get energy.

It's something just as amazing as photosynthesis, and it shocked scientists— who had to rethink their entire understanding of how life-forms survive.

It's called chemosynthesis (key-mo-SIN-thuh-sis).

BREAK IT DOWN
CHEMOSYNTHESIS

Chemo- = chemical
-synthesis = put together

CHEMOSYNTHESIS
CAFÉ
TRY OUR HOMEMADE
methane!

OPEN

Instead of starting with plants or algae, down here life begins with specialized bacteria. They can turn chemicals like hydrogen sulfide, methane, and hydrogen into energy! And since these are the same chemicals spewing out of hydrothermal vents, these chemosynthesizing bacteria have plenty to nosh on! It's a never-ending feast at the Chemosynthesis Café!

These microscopic bacteria form the bottom of the deep-sea food chain. They are eaten by small creatures, who are then eaten by bigger ones…and those are eaten by even bigger ones…and on and on. This allows all kinds of critters to exist in a place where we used to think it was impossible to survive.

MEET THE LOCALS

Check out who's chilling at the hydrothermal vents!

Tube worms can grow up to six and a half feet long and have no mouths. We're not sure which fact is creepier!

Mussels like to cluster in groups around the vents. They hold on with their strong grip, really putting the *muscle* in *mussels*.

ANSWER!

It's a hydrothermal vent called a black smoker—it's like a chimney that spews out superheated water. The water is full of tiny particles of a mineral called iron sulfide, which gives it that black color. When the heated water from the hydrothermal vent hits the colder deep-sea water, the iron sulfide particles become solid. That causes the water flowing from the hydrothermal vent to appear darker than the water around it.

This **ocean dandelion** is no flower—it's a group of minuscule creatures that grab on to one another with l-o-n-g tentacles and search the ocean floor for dead stuff to eat. *Nom nom nom!*

Yeti crabs are covered in hairy, white bristles, making them look like a tiny version of the Abominable Snowman. They like to eat the bacteria that grow in their hair, which is both super convenient and super gross.

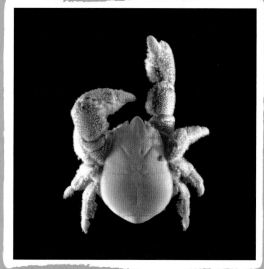

DEEP, DEEP WATERS

Oceans cover more than two-thirds of the earth's surface…yet humans have explored only about 5 percent of these wondrous waters.

Clothes cover more than two-thirds of my room. One of these days, I'm going to explore a path to the washing machine.

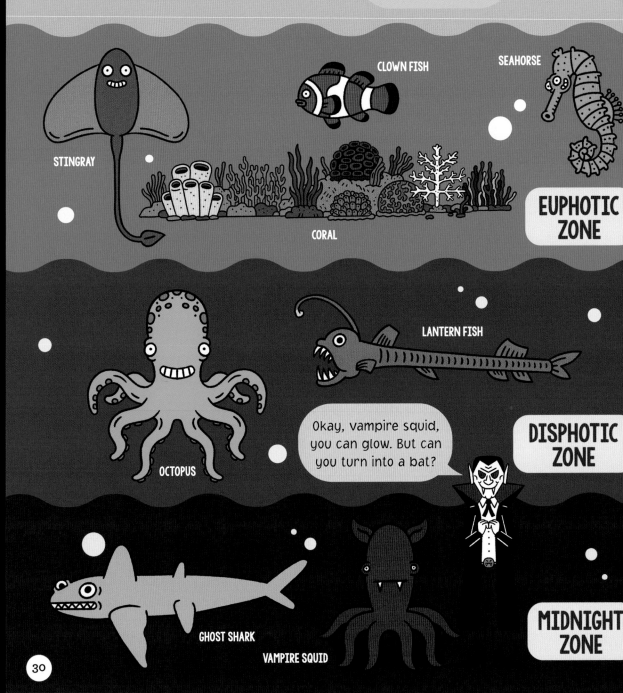

CLOWN FISH

SEAHORSE

STINGRAY

CORAL

EUPHOTIC ZONE

LANTERN FISH

OCTOPUS

Okay, vampire squid, you can glow. But can you turn into a bat?

DISPHOTIC ZONE

GHOST SHARK

VAMPIRE SQUID

MIDNIGHT ZONE

We don't know how many species live down there, but scientists discover new creatures all the time.

Part of the reason oceans are tricky to explore is that they not only cover so much of the surface of our planet—they go deep too.

The euphotic zone, or sunlight zone, is the top layer. The name says it all: It's where light from the sun pierces through the water. It's where we swim on beach days. It's where plants, like seaweed, grow. And it's where many incredible and beautiful sea creatures dwell, from coral and clown fish to seahorses and stingrays.

The next layer is called the disphotic zone, or twilight zone. Less light reaches this level of the ocean, so plants can't grow here. It's not completely dark, though, and many ocean creatures live here happily, like lantern fish and viperfish. Keep an eye out for bright sparks of bioluminescence too!

Dive a little deeper (with the appropriate equipment, of course!), and you'll find yourself in the midnight zone.

BREAK IT DOWN
EUPHOTIC ZONE

Eu- = good

-photic = light

zone = belt

DISPHOTIC ZONE

Dis- = bad

-photic = light

zone = belt

Creatures in the midnight zone like their ocean like I like my coffee: dark! No cream, no sugar.

Darker than the darkest night you can imagine—not a ray of sunlight reaches the waters of the midnight zone. But that doesn't keep strange and wondrous creatures from living their best lives here. All kinds of incredible life-forms have evolved to thrive in the midnight zone—from the ghost shark to the vampire squid. Seems like the deeper we go, the more creatures sound like monsters from scary movies.

Way to Glow!

At depths like these—thousands of feet below the surface—no sunlight can penetrate the water. It's pitch-black. But wait, what was that? A flicker of light! There's another one! And another! Flashes of blue…green…red…it's an incredible sight to behold. Is it an underwater dance party? No, it's just bioluminescent creatures. Bioluminescence is the ability of some animals to produce their own light.

These underwater light shows can really come in handy. Some sea creatures sparkle like a strand of twinkling lights to lure their prey toward them. Then—CHOMP! Dinner is served!

Others use bioluminescence to escape from being eaten. An unexpected flash of bright light can scare away predators. And some creatures that glow don't even do it on their own. They light up thanks to thousands of itsy-bitsy bioluminescent bacteria inside their bodies. Shine on, you beautiful beasts!

Trench Talk

The very deepest parts of the ocean are called trenches. They are extremely narrow, extraordinarily deep cracks in the ocean floor that are caused by the movement of the tectonic plates (you know, pieces of the earth's crust—check out page 7 for more about the crust).

In these trenches, the water temperature hovers near freezing. There is no light, which means no plants. And hydrostatic pressure is more than 1,000 times the pressure we feel just hanging out on the surface of the earth. That's like fifty jumbo

FACT-ASTIC VOYAGE

The Mariana Trench is the deepest spot on earth. Located in the Pacific Ocean, it bottoms out at 35,814 feet. That's nearly seven miles below sea level. If you moved Mount Everest, the tallest mountain on earth, to the bottom of the Mariana Trench, it wouldn't even get close to the surface!

jets stacked on a person! Yet even here, life finds a way! These murky depths are home to bizarro beasts such as pale, shrimplike amphipods and sluglike creatures called sea cucumbers.

Road Trip SOUVENIR

SNAILFISH SELFIES

Say cheese! Of all the strange and wonderful creatures in the ocean, the snailfish deserves a special prize. There are more than 350 species of snailfish found in oceans around the world, but a unique variety of snailfish was discovered in the Mariana Trench in 2014. These snailfish are so transparent you can see their guts right through their skin! They might also be the deepest-dwelling fish on the entire planet. So if you're lucky enough to spot one of these rare beauties, be sure to grab a selfie!

Extra, Extra! Monsters of the Deep!

For centuries, people have been fascinated—and horrified—at the thought of sea monsters. From the mighty kraken to the fearsome Leviathan, many different cultures have legends about impossibly big creatures from the depths of the sea. But is there any truth to these tall tales? Could there really be enormous creatures lurking beneath the ocean's surface?

As it turns out, the answer is yes!

Thanks to a strange phenomenon called deep-sea gigantism, sea creatures that live at the deepest level of the ocean can grow to be extraordinarily large. Think of the colossal squid (the giant squid's even bigger cousin, pictured right), which can grow to forty-six feet long. That's as big as a full-size school bus! Or picture the giant oarfish, which can tip the scales at 600 pounds.

 Good thing they don't have feet. Where would you find shoes that size?!

But why do these sea beasts get so big? Scientists have a few ideas.

Without sunlight, the depths of the ocean get awfully dark—and awfully cold. As a result, a creature's cells grow bigger than usual and it can live a longer life—which means more years for growth. Another theory has to do with food. Food is hard to find down below, and the bigger you are, the easier it is to swim long distances looking for it. Or maybe these animals get so big because there are almost no predators to eat them. After all, if you don't have to hide from your enemies, why not grow to be large and in charge?

With massively monstrous sea creatures dwelling at the bottom of the ocean, do you need to worry about them when you splash around at the shore?

Nope!

Good old hydrostatic pressure keeps them deep down below.

If they tried to reach the higher ocean elevations, such as the euphotic zone, their bodies would basically explode from the change in pressure. So instead of a gigantic creature, you'd just see a gigantic mess. The good news is you don't have to worry about running into a giant squid the next time you catch some waves! The bad news is you'll never get to see a giant squid try to ride a surfboard.

DEEP-SEA EXPLORATION: SWAN DIVES AND BELLY FLOPS

The mysterious depths of the sea have been calling to humans for thousands of years—but people can only go so deep on their own. A scuba diving world record was recently set at just over 1,000 feet! But even with the right gear, most people shouldn't try to go deeper than 130 feet. Why? Two words: hydrostatic pressure.

The Pressure's On!

Life is full of pressure, like the pressure you feel when you're about to take a test or the pressure to look cool in front of your crush. But the hydrostatic pressure you feel

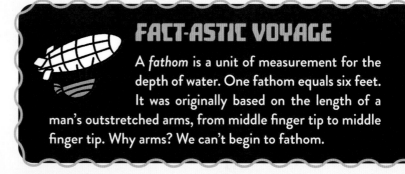

FACT-ASTIC VOYAGE

A *fathom* is a unit of measurement for the depth of water. One fathom equals six feet. It was originally based on the length of a man's outstretched arms, from middle finger tip to middle finger tip. Why arms? We can't begin to fathom.

when you're submerged deep in the ocean is something else entirely. As you swim down, there's more water between you and the surface. Since more water means more weight, the pressure grows and pushes against you on all sides. *Yowch!* Hydrostatic pressure can even kill you if you dive too deep without gear to protect you.

So how in the world did humans find a way to explore the deepest parts of the ocean? Well, we did what we do best! Pet dogs and eat pizza! Wait, that's not right. We used science!

MYSTERY PHOTO

Focus your eyes on this mystery photo. Can you guess what it is? Turn to page 38 for the answer!

GREAT MOMENTS IN DEEP-SEA EXPLORATION

HMS *CHALLENGER*
(1872–1876)

This research boat set out to measure the depth of the ocean with a heavy lead weight that was attached to a very long piece of rope. Every 140 miles they traveled, the crew tossed the weight overboard. When it hit the bottom of the ocean, the crew measured the rope to calculate the depth. But something unexpected happened in 1875, when the weight kept dropping...and dropping...and dropping. Eventually the crew recorded a depth of 4,475 fathoms, or about five miles.

BATHYSPHERE
(1934)

Explorer William Beebe longed to explore the ocean depths, but all his attempts at creating a submersible failed. Then engineer Otis Barton invented the bathysphere, a spherical seacraft that took Beebe and Barton more than half a mile below the surface (3,028 feet, to be exact)—shattering the previous record of 383 feet!

BATHYSCAPHE *TRIESTE*
(1960)

Oceanographers and explorers Jacques Piccard and Don Walsh used a submersible called the bathyscaphe *Trieste* to reach the deepest part of the Mariana Trench—more than 35,800 feet below sea level! When Piccard and Walsh reached the ocean floor, their submersible kicked up such a cloud of debris that they couldn't see much out the window. Soon after, our old frenemy hydrostatic pressure caused the window to crack, which forced them to return to the surface! Their record-breaking trip was cut short just twenty minutes after they landed.

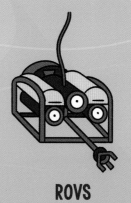

ROVS
(REMOTELY OPERATED VEHICLES)

For more than fifty years after the *Trieste*'s trip, the only exploration of the Mariana Trench was done by ROVs, or remotely operated vehicles. These deep-sea diving robots were controlled by researchers from the safety of the surface and helped us to understand much more about the mysteries of the deep.

DEEPSEA CHALLENGER
(2012)

Humanity's greatest deep-sea success came in 2012, when filmmaker James Cameron took the plunge. Cameron had been fascinated by the deep sea for a long time, and he even made blockbuster movies about it. He crammed himself into a submersible called the *Deepsea Challenger* and traveled on his own into the Mariana Trench, breaking the record for the deepest solo trip ever when he went deeper than 35,700 feet! Cameron's trip was a big success in other ways too. He was able to spend a few hours exploring the Mariana Trench, making observations and collecting samples. *Trench-mendous!*

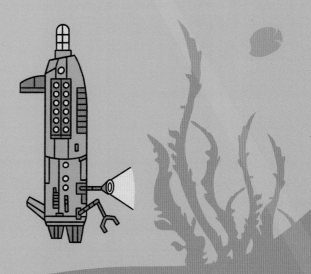

ANSWER!

That's a cuttlefish! Cuttlefish and other cephalopods can change the color and texture of their skin to blend in with their surroundings. Great for deep-sea hide-and-seek!

THE ADVENTURES OF BEEBE AND BARTON

Meet William Beebe, an explorer.

Beebe wanted to design an underwater seacraft. But all his ideas...sank.

Meet Otis Barton, an engineer. He had some new ideas.

It's a SPHERE! The ocean pressure won't crush it!

Beebe and Barton became partners—but not exactly friends.

Even worse, Barton got seasick!

It's the BATHYSPHERE, not the BARFYSPHERE!

On August 15, 1934, after lots of false starts...

SPLASH!

...they descended 3,028 feet, shattering all previous records!

Beebe and Barton changed our understanding of the ocean forever.

Tour the Bathysphere: It's a Tight Fit!

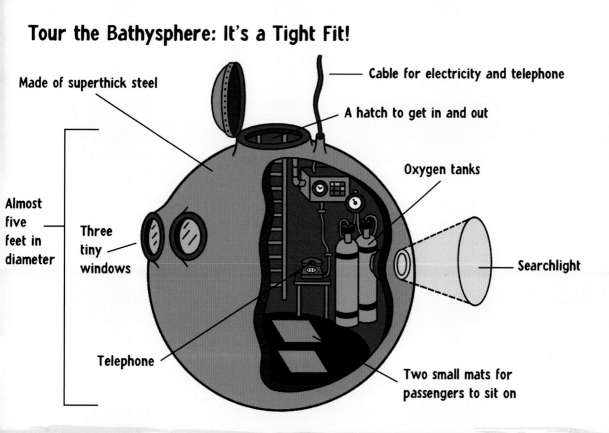

Made of superthick steel

Cable for electricity and telephone

A hatch to get in and out

Oxygen tanks

Almost five feet in diameter

Three tiny windows

Searchlight

Telephone

Two small mats for passengers to sit on

PIT STOP

MUSA

MUSA, or Museo Subacuático de Arte, is the largest underwater museum in the world. Located in the waters of Cancún, Mexico, it features hundreds of underwater sculptures. You can snorkel, scuba dive, or glide around on a glass-bottom boat to view the exhibits.

MUSA isn't just interesting—it's important too. All the tourists who visited the fragile coral reefs around Cancún were inadvertently damaging these vital habitats. MUSA was constructed to give underwater visitors a safe way to explore the world beneath the waves.

Best of all, the sculptures at MUSA were specially designed to support the formation of new coral reefs. Covered in algae and coral, the structures are drawing fish to the exhibits and creating a wonderful new habitat for some of the ocean's most eye-catching creatures.

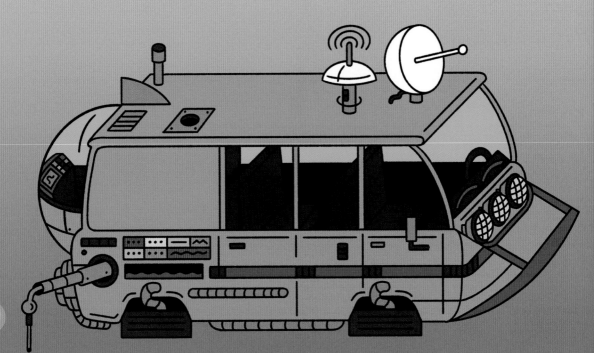

EXPLORERR MAKEOVERR

Extreme can be exciting, but we can all breathe a sigh of relief now that we're heading to the surface and leaving behind extreme temps and extreme pressure.

LOSING	ADDING
✔ Capsule-shaped shell	✔ Water-quality testing station
✔ Fins	✔ Jet Ski propulsion system
	✔ Retractable wheels

VISIT THE *Hydrothermal* *Vents**

*WARNING: Do not visit the hydrothermal vents without appropriate protective gear. Do not touch the superheated water. Do not drink the chemical- and bacteria-filled water. Actually, maybe you should visit somewhere else instead!

Hi, Friend!

Our trip to the deep sea is just about done, and all we can say is W-O-W! It's truly incredible down here—and a little freaky. Just look up "giant tube worms" or "vampire squid" sometime. Anyway, we can't wait to find out more about the mysteries of the ocean. There's a lot to learn, a lot to discover, and a lot to explore down here. You might say we've barely scratched the surface, er, the bottom!

Splish splash!

Molly, Marc, and Sanden

You, Yes YOU

Reading This Now

Earth, Milky Way

Surf's up, and so are we! We're finally free from the crushing depths of the deep sea. Now it's time to relax and ride the tides! Waves are fun to play in, but don't be fooled—these beauties can also be extremely powerful. Sometimes they flood beach towns or turn into terrible tsunamis that wipe out entire coastlines. Let's wade into the science behind these wet wonders.

TIDES: THE MOTION OF THE OCEAN

Ocean tides start—believe it or not—in space! Aliens made them, because it turns out they love to sail! Just kidding. Tides are actually made by the moon! The moon has a powerful impact on the oceans, thanks to the force of…*dun dun dun*…GRAVITY!

The gravitational force of the moon is constantly pulling on the earth, which means it can be felt all over our planet. The effect is small, so you don't notice it. But you know what *does* notice? Water. Since water moves easily, that gravitational pull makes the ocean rise, creating a bulge in the area under the moon. Since water likes to move to positions where all the forces on it are balanced, this actually causes two bulges of water. One is on the side of the earth facing the moon, and the other is on the opposite side.

Is that tide following me? I feel like it's following me.

Another way to describe that bulge: high tide!

The bulging of high tide follows the moon and moves around the planet as the earth rotates. When the moon is in its new phase, meaning it's between the earth and the sun and looks mostly invisible in the sky, the gravity from the sun adds an extra boost to that effect. It's like the sun is helping the moon pull even more on those tides. This makes high tide even higher and low tide even lower. That's some tidal teamwork!

WHAT ABOUT WAVES?

When you see your BFF and wiggle your hand at them, that's a wave. When a bunch of people at a stadium stand up and raise their arms at the same time, that's also a wave. And when powerful winds blow across the ocean, causing the water to rise and fall, that too is a wave.

NEWTON SAYS!

The gravitational force between two bodies is proportional to the mass of each body and inversely proportional to the square of the distance between their centers, and the force is directed along the line between the centers of the objects.

What he means is that the gravitational pull between two objects is stronger the closer, and heavier, they are.

The stronger the wind, the bigger the waves. And really big, monster waves come from really big, monster winds. As waves travel across the water, they don't lose much energy. So the mega-waves you see at the beach may have come from a mega-storm far out at sea.

The shape of waves close to shore, on the other hand, doesn't come from the surface of the water. Instead, it's influenced by the bottom of the ocean. Where the water

OTHER CAUSES OF WAVES

There are a few other natural phenomena that can create waves. The shuddering and shaking of an underwater earthquake can make some whopper waves, including dangerous tsunamis. An underwater landslide can do the same. And when big meteors fall from the sky and hit the ocean, that can send water *whooshing* to the shore!

gets shallow, the energy of the wave starts to interact with the ocean floor. That causes a drag on the bottom of the wave that slows it down, while the top of the wave keeps cruising along. The result is those awesome curving, crashing wave shapes we know and love.

My patented gut-busting belly flop also causes some pretty serious waves. Watch out!

So, to put it another way...Waves are mostly caused by wind blowing across the water. Tides are caused by the gravitational force of the moon and, to a lesser extent, the sun.

And if you're at the beach waving at tides, you might get strange looks.

Keep it weird, pal

TOTAL TIDAL TEAM UP

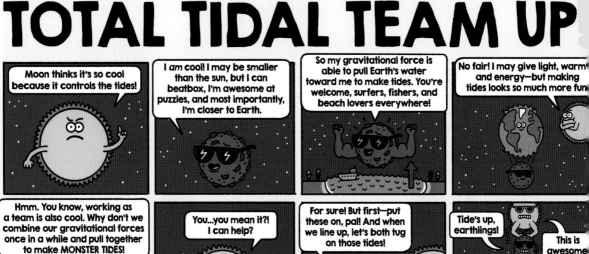

Moon thinks it's so cool because it controls the tides!

I *am* cool! I may be smaller than the sun, but I can beatbox, I'm awesome at puzzles, and most importantly, I'm closer to Earth.

So my gravitational force is able to pull Earth's water toward me to make tides. You're welcome, surfers, fishers, and beach lovers everywhere!

No fair! I may give light, warmth and energy—but making tides looks so much more fun

Hmm. You know, working as a team is also cool. Why don't we combine our gravitational forces once in a while and pull together to make MONSTER TIDES!

You...you mean it?! I can help?

For sure! But first—put these on, pal! And when we line up, let's both tug on those tides!

Tide's up, earthlings!

This is awesome

FACT-ASTIC VOYAGE

When a wave breaks, air gets trapped in it and forms tiny bubbles. Those bubbles make the wave look white at the edges when it's crashing down. And the sound of a wave crashing? That's the noise the bubbles make when they pop! Waves: the seltzer of the sea!

SALTY, SALTY OCEAN

Have you ever accidentally swallowed a mouthful of seawater? Blech! So salty! Who is seasoning this thing? It turns out it's nature's chefs—lakes, rivers, and rocks.

Take a lick—whoops! We mean, take a *look* at this rock. You wouldn't think it's salty, would you? In fact, this rock—and all rocks—are full of different minerals. Over time, the rocks and soil at the edges of rivers and lakes break down. This process is called erosion.

As the minerals dissolve into the river or lake, they are carried through the water. BUT WAIT! Rivers and lakes aren't salty like the ocean—right? Well, it turns out that they *are* a little salty—just not nearly as salty as ocean water.

Since lakes and rivers usually flow out to sea, they eventually pour their slightly salty water into the ocean. But the ocean doesn't have anywhere to dump its salty water, so the salt just builds and builds! Then the forces of evaporation supercharge the saltiness. You see, as ocean water evaporates and

Salt contains sodium, which is essential for the functioning of human cells because it helps create a conductive solution that promotes cellular communication through the use of electrical signals.

I mean, ARRRRRR. Salt be important for ya!

KNOW YOUR SALTS

Salt. Without it, food is bland. Too much, and food is inedible. But if you add the right amount, it can make just about everything taste better. It's like the Goldilocks of seasonings!

If the salt you use for cooking is called sea salt, that means it likely comes from the ocean. Salty ocean water is gathered in shallow ponds, and when the water evaporates, salt crystals are left behind. Other table salt is mined from underground salt deposits, which were left there by bodies of salty water that have since dried up.

goes into the air, the salt is left behind. So over time, more and more salt builds up, like one massive spilled saltshaker.

So why isn't the ocean nothing but salt at this point? Well, luckily salts are being removed from the ocean through a process called mineral precipitation. That means some of those dissolved minerals that make up salt come out of the water and become solids again, like rocks.

It's a whole cycle, making the ocean like a complicated machine that carefully balances just how salty it is!

I wish Marc could learn this salt balancing trick. Have you tried his soups? Blech!

H₂OHHH YEAH!

Like E.T., Chewbacca, and Mr. Spock, water is an interstellar traveler. It formed way out in the final frontier of space and came to earth with a bang!

But before we talk about that, let's get to know the water molecule. It likes long swims at the beach and traveling through straws, and it's probably an Aquarius, right? Water is made up of two elements: hydrogen and oxygen. Have you ever heard someone call water H_2O? That abbreviation means two hydrogen (H) atoms and one oxygen (O) atom. It's the not-so-secret recipe for water. But to really understand where water comes from, we have to go way, way, *way* back in time.

Let's start at the beginning—the very beginning—the origin of the universe. When the big bang happened, it scattered lots of material, most of which was the element hydrogen. There was some helium too.

So we had hydrogen, one of the key ingredients for H_2O. But did we have water? Nope. Not yet. Next we needed oxygen. That came later.

Over time, that helium and hydrogen combined to form stars, like our sun. Stars burn hydrogen at super hot temperatures, like a giant oven that cooks up lots of other elements, including oxygen. (For more on this, visit page 4.)

Really big stars burn quickly, and when they burn out, they explode. It's called a supernova, and it scatters all sorts of newly formed elements into the universe. Hydrogen, oxygen, and everything else that was made in the star can now combine into different molecules, including water. Finally, we have H_2O!

But how did that water go from stuff in space to covering the earth's surface?

Scientists think that about 4.5 billion years ago, when our planet was formed, it was made out of all sorts of floating space material—including water molecules. And over time, lots and lots of comets hit the planet. Those comets brought even more H_2O to earth. Eventually, our planet had enough wet stuff to form lakes, rivers, and oceans. So the next time you take a dip in a pool, give a shout-out to the stars and comets that made it all possible!

HOLA, EL NIÑO!

Fishermen in Peru were the first to notice a bizarre phenomenon. Some years, the water off the coast would get warmer than usual and there would be fewer fish. Strange…but then things got stranger! Unusual storms would hit the land and turn deserts into lush fields of grass. It was like Opposite Day in weather-land! What was happening? This odd trend usually started around Christmastime, so the people dubbed it El Niño, which is how they referred to baby Jesus in the story of Christmas.

Decades later, scientists discovered that El Niño didn't just affect Peru. It affected the ENTIRE WORLD! It turns out the water off the coast of Peru is like a switch. When it is activated, it sets off a chain reaction of wild, unusual weather events around the world. Some places get hit with intense storms or cold weather; other places face heat and punishing droughts.

Here's how it works: Usually, winds over the Pacific Ocean push warm water at the surface toward the west. It's kind of like Mother Nature is blowing on a bowl of soup to cool it off. That wind moves the warm water farther out to the ocean, letting the colder water from below rise up. This keeps the coastal water relatively cool.

Some years, though, those winds are weaker than normal, so the warm water stays put and builds up. That's when things get interesting. More and more rain clouds form over all that warm water. These storms eventually get blown to other places, leading to heavy rains in parts of South America and the southeastern United States. This can cause serious flooding and force some people to flee their homes. In other

LA NIÑA

La Niña—or "the girl" in Spanish—causes the opposite effects of El Niño. La Niña's strong winds blow from east to west, making the ocean temperature colder than usual. During La Niña, areas that get more rain with El Niño systems have much drier weather—while those that have droughts from El Niño experience rainy conditions.

places, like southern Africa and parts of California, rain disappears, causing dangerous droughts. These effects can last a whole year.

We can't stop El Niño, but we've gotten much better at tracking it. Scientists can use satellites up in space to measure the temperature of oceans and follow unusual storms that develop. It's a powerful reminder that no matter how good our technology is, we're still at the mercy of Mother Nature. So make sure you have your raincoat handy!

GULF STREAM GETAWAY

On the surface, oceans look like just a bunch of water floating around with no real plan. But in reality, there are parts where the water is cruising along like cars on a highway! We call these areas currents, and they affect weather around the world. One of the most famous is the Gulf Stream.

The Gulf Stream stretches from the Gulf of Mexico through the Atlantic Ocean, up to Canada and Europe. It's like a humongous conveyor belt carrying warm water from those southern areas up north. It's not super fast; on average, water in the Gulf Stream moves only about four miles an hour. But it moves A LOT of water—nearly 4 billion cubic feet per second! That's more water than the amount carried by all the world's rivers *combined*!

That massive movement of warm water has an equally massive impact on global temperatures. Many countries in Europe should be much colder according to their position on the globe. For example, England should be as cold as Canada

FACT-ASTIC VOYAGE

Humans have observed the effects of the Gulf Stream for more than 500 years! Explorer Juan Ponce de León was the first to record it. Then sailors realized they could travel along the current of the Gulf Stream to reach their destination more quickly. Benjamin Franklin was the first person to map the Gulf Stream. He named it too!

(*brrr!*). But thanks to the waters of the Gulf Stream, which release warmth into the atmosphere, England doesn't get nearly as chilly as Canada.

LIQUID AWESOMENESS!

Imagine, if you will, a substance that defies nature. That can crawl upward against gravity. That's both sticky AND slippery, hard AND soft, able to cut through the toughest rock, yet can be moved by a gentle wind. What is this alien substance? A thing created in some secret lab?

Nah, it's just water. Let's get to know this mind-blowing substance a little bit better.

A Magnificent Molecule

Water is one of the most amazing things in the entire universe! To understand why, we need to look at what it is made of. Water is a molecule. It's made up of ultra-tiny things called atoms. Specifically, a water molecule is a combination of two hydrogen atoms and one oxygen atom. That's why it's sometimes called H_2O. Sounds simple enough, right? Well, when these little atoms get together, fantastic things happen!

The weirdness of water is thanks to the forces that hold these oxygen and hydrogen atoms together. You see, every oxygen atom has a small negative charge, and the two hydrogen atoms have an even smaller positive charge. Just like with the negative and positive ends of magnets, the negatively charged oxygen atom and positively charged hydrogen atoms want to stick together. Opposites attract, right? It's that attraction that holds the atoms of a water molecule together.

So that's how a single water molecule is built. But the attractions don't stop there. It turns out that each water molecule also has a slightly positive side and a slightly negative side. So what do you think happens when you put several water molecules in the same space?

The negative side of one water molecule grabs on to the positive side of another water molecule. Basically, the molecules start clinging to one another—like a bunch of friends at a party all holding hands! That's why when you spill water on the counter it sticks together in little droplets. Water molecules like to stay close to one another.

Hooray for the Hydrogen Bond!

There's a special name for these attractions that help water molecules stick together: hydrogen bonds. In the world of chemistry, these bonds are very important because they form only between hydrogen atoms and other charged molecules. They are weaker than the bonds that hold the atoms within each individual water molecule together. It's like the difference between a firm, long-lasting handshake (which is like the attraction that holds the atoms in a single water molecule together) and a quick, passing high five (which is like the bonds that hold several water molecules together).

Another important thing to know about hydrogen bonds is that they exist for only a fraction of a second. In other words, your glass of water is actually filled with many water molecules that are zooming around high-fiving one another as their hydrogen bonds form, dissolve, and form again.

FACT-ASTIC VOYAGE

Those sticky hydrogen bonds are the reason that water can make other things, like your hair, wet. Wet hair is the result of water molecules sticking to your hair molecules.

The 411 on Frozen H$_2$O

Another incredible thing about water is that it expands when it freezes. Why is that incredible? Well, most liquids contract, or get smaller, when they freeze. But not water!

As water cools, those high-fiving hydrogen bonds start lasting longer and longer until they finally freeze in place. This forces water molecules to be farther apart than they were in their liquid state. Remember those hydrogen bond high fives? When water freezes, each outstretched arm gets stuck, leaving more room between the molecules and making ice less dense than liquid water.

When most things freeze, they sink in the liquid version of themselves. But if you've ever watched ice cubes bob around in your drink, you know that water does its own thing! The fact that ice floats prevents creatures that live in the water from freezing to death in cold weather. Ice on top of rivers and lakes is like a blanket that protects the deeper parts from the cold. So if any fish are reading this, you should thank ice for keeping you from becoming a fish-cicle!

Defying Gravity

Like Spider-Man, water is an excellent climber. That's because the same hydrogen bonds that help water molecules stick together

Move it on up!

help them stick to other surfaces as well. If you look very closely at a glass of water, you'll see that the edge of the water curves up slightly. That's because water is sticking to the side of the glass. If you transformed that glass into a very thin, very narrow tube, you'd actually be able to see water travel *up* the side of the tube. This is how water flows from the roots of a tree up to the leafy crown.

TRY IT!

Want to see water's gravity-defying power in action? Fill a glass of water halfway. Then dip a piece of paper towel in the water (make sure part of the paper towel sticks out of the glass). What do you think will happen next?

The Superb Solvent

A solvent is something that can break down other things—and water is one of the best solvents around. That's why it's perfect for cleaning—it can break up messy materials, like dried ketchup on the counter or crusty mud on the floor. In fact, water can dissolve almost anything, given enough time! Think of the Grand Canyon. It exists because of the incredible solvent powers of water. Millions of years of flowing water carved the enormous channels that created this natural marvel. By the way, water, you're a marvelous sculptor.

THE WATER CYCLE

Water is the *only* natural substance on earth that exists in all three different states: solid (like ice), gas (like steam), and liquid (like, uh, liquid water). As water changes between its different forms in nature, it's constantly going through a process called the water cycle. The same water moves from clouds to rain to lakes and rivers, and then back to clouds, where the process starts all over again.

Here's how it goes.

First, the sun shines down on oceans, lakes, and rivers, making the water evaporate. Plants also sweat their water into the air through a process called transpiration. Now liquid water has become water vapor, which floats into the sky. As the vapor rises higher and higher, it gets colder, which causes it to condense and form into clouds. The clouds then make rain and snow, sending water back to earth to fill the oceans, lakes, and rivers (as well as nourishing plants). Then the cycle begins again—and again—and again. In fact, it never ends. It's basically nature's recycling plant for water, which means the water we depend on for life has been moving through the water cycle for millions of years.

BREAK IT DOWN
EVAPORATION

E- = out of

-vaporation = change into gas

TRANSPIRATION

Trans- = through

-piration = to breathe

FACT-ASTIC VOYAGE

Did you know we drink the same water that dinosaurs drank long, long ago? It's true—and all thanks to the water cycle!

SPECIAL AGENT H₂O: Fighting crime with the superpowers of WATER

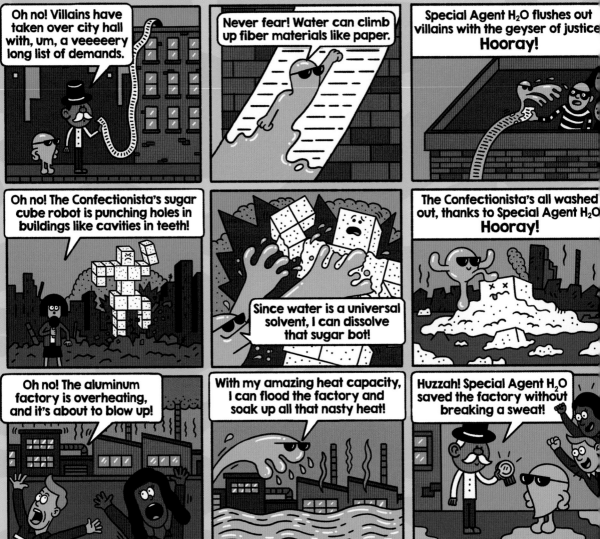

RIVERS AND LAKES

We love sailing the oh-so-salty seas, but now it's time to explore some other bodies of water. We're talking lakes and rivers! We call these freshwater sources because they're typically not as salty as an ocean. They're also the perfect place to spend a lazy afternoon on a hot summer's day. So let's dive in and meet our freshwater friends!

Lakes can be shallow or deep; as small as a pond or as big as a sea. Some lakes were created when giant, icy glaciers melted. Others were formed in the craters of old volcanoes. The movement of tectonic plates can make cracks or faults that eventually fill with water and become lakes too. We love all lakes, so we find no fault in that!

Rivers use the force of gravity to flow downhill, and they can pick up pebbles and rocks, as well as salts and minerals, along the way. Sometimes rivers flow through wetlands, which slows them down and gives plants the chance to clean pollution from them (thanks, plants!).

Creeks and streams are simply names for smaller rivers. Some are short or shallow; others are wide or deep. Often a series of creeks and streams will feed into a larger river.

MEGA MATCHUP

NILE VS. LAKE SUPERIOR

Time to take sides as the Nile River and Lake Superior battle for coolest body of water! In one corner, the Nile River (beware the bite of the Nile crocodile)! And in the other corner, Lake Superior (watch out for treacherous storms)! Which waterway will reign supreme—and which one is all washed up?

TEAM NILE RIVER

- The Nile River is the longest river in the world, measuring more than 4,000 miles. It flows through eleven different countries in Africa: Egypt, Sudan, South Sudan, Ethiopia, Eritrea, Rwanda, Kenya, Burundi, Tanzania, Uganda, and the Democratic Republic of the Congo.

- The Nile River has been essential to humans for more than 5,000 years. When it flooded every August, it was possible for people to grow food in an area that otherwise would've been a dry and dusty desert.

- The Nile River and its banks are an important habitat for reptiles, fish, and other animals, including the ferocious Nile crocodile, one of the world's largest reptiles.

- A river as awesome as the Nile deserves an awesome holiday, don't you think? Wafaa an-Nil is a two-week holiday that Egyptians celebrate every year.

- More than 95 percent of Egyptians get their water from the Nile. The country would be uninhabitable without it.

TEAM LAKE SUPERIOR

- Lake Superior is the largest lake in the United States, measuring more than 31,000 square miles. It's larger than twelve of the fifty states, including Maine and South Carolina.

- Of all the Great Lakes, Lake Superior is definitely...superior. You could fit all the water from the other Great Lakes inside it!

- Lake Superior contains 10 percent of the entire planet's freshwater supply!

- Surf's up! The highest wave recorded at Lake Superior measured about thirty feet. No wonder it's a popular spot for surfers to catch a wave!

- Lake Superior is no stranger to danger. Powerful storms often sweep over it, sinking many a ship. There have been more than 350 shipwrecks there.

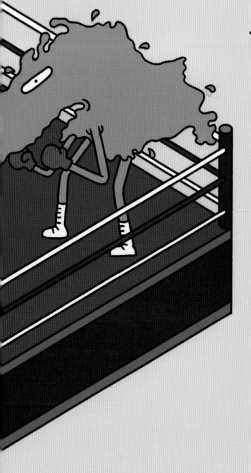

Which body
of water is cooler:
Nile River or
Lake Superior?

YOUR VERDICT

POISONED WATERS AND RIVERS OF FIRE

Rivers do so much for us. They give us water to drink, fish to eat, and a place to swim. We can row small boats on them or float giant cargo ships. We can even build dams on them to harness their power and turn it into electricity. Given how useful rivers are, you'd think we'd treat them like a BFF. Instead, for decades, we treated them like a dump. At one point, it got so bad that some rivers frequently caught on fire!

Case Study: The Cuyahoga River

For a long time, one of the main sources of river pollution in the United States was factories. They were often built on riverbanks, and they would use the water as a place to dump their waste. That's what happened to the Cuyahoga River in Ohio, one of the most notoriously filthy rivers in history.

The pollution in the Cuyahoga River was so bad that when researchers did a study to learn how many fish could survive in such dirty water, they found only two species of fish in a forty-five-mile stretch of the river. The river was too toxic for most fish to survive.

So where did all that pollution come from—and how did it lead to a burning river? There were several factors. Raw sewage flowed in from cities and contaminated the river. Let's be clear: "Raw sewage" means the stuff from your toilets (GROSS!). Paint companies added to the pollution when cleaning out their paint tanks, which let pigments flow into the river. All kinds of debris (like lumber and branches) as well as trash (like plastic and junk) filled up the river too. Worst of all, though, was the oil pollution.

Sometimes oil from the refinery would spill into the river and soak into the debris that piled up. Since the Cuyahoga was a slow-moving river, that debris didn't travel very fast—or very far. When it soaked up the oil, it became flammable. All it took was a spark, and *whoosh!*

The pile of oil-soaked debris—and the Cuyahoga—would start to burn.

It happened several times during the twentieth century, but it wasn't until June 22, 1969, that people finally said enough was enough.

The whole country knew it was time for a big change.

Saving the Cuyahoga

There's an old saying—"the solution to pollution is dilution," which basically means that with enough water, toxic stuff will spread out so much that it won't be a problem anymore. That's one reason people used to think it would be fine to dump anything into a river.

Unfortunately, they were wrong. Slow-moving rivers like the Cuyahoga can't just rinse all that bad stuff through them very easily.

Enter the *Putzfrau*.

Putzfrau means "cleaning lady" in German

The *Putzfrau* was a cleaning boat, and it was one of the first to start tidying up the river. It would glide along, collecting debris and vacuuming oil spills off the water. The *Putzfrau* could clean 15,000 gallons of oil in one day. Amazing! But that still meant that the *Putzfrau* was needed on the Cuyahoga River several days a week, for many years. If a polluter was caught by the Coast Guard, they were forced to pay for the cleanup. If not, the Coast Guard paid for it.

It was clear to everyone that more help was needed in the United States. So, in 1970, the country formed the Environmental Protection Agency (EPA). Its job was to study and monitor the environment. Two years after that, Congress passed the Clean Water Act.

Now the EPA had the power to set standards for what could and couldn't be dumped into waterways. And that was great news for rivers all over the country. "Hooray!" they said. Actually, the rivers said nothing because they are rivers. Still, it was good news. Now, more than fifty years after the Cuyahoga's last fire, it's clean enough that people can actually enjoy spending time there again. It's not perfectly pristine; there's still more cleanup to do. But the good news is that all sorts of fish, bugs, and birds have returned—including creatures like the smallmouth bass that are especially sensitive to pollution. The river is healing—and people are helping.

Road Trip SOUVENIR

AN OLD BALL

Normally, we'd never take something from a natural habitat, but in this case, we'll gladly make an exception. One of the big pollutants of the Cuyahoga River was balls—the kind that kids play with. When storms happened, sometimes balls that had been left behind on the sidewalk or the street would roll into the gutters and get flushed out to the Cuyahoga. Once they hit the river, those balls just slowly bobbed along, joining with other debris to form floating mats of junk. Yuck! Better to have this in our souvenir collection than floating in a river!

SUPER COOL SCIENTIST

GITANJALI RAO

Gitanjali Rao isn't just a super cool scientist—she's a super young scientist too. When Gitanjali was eleven years old, she won the 2017 Discovery Education 3M Young Scientist Challenge for an invention that helps people learn more about their water. The invention is called Tethys, named after the Greek goddess of fresh water, and can easily detect whether lead is in a water sample. This is important because if people drink water that has lead in it, they can get sick! Gitanjali is still inventing today and is working on a new device that will detect other contaminants in water, to make sure everyone has access to clean water. In 2020, Gitanjali was named the first-ever Kid of the Year by *Time* magazine in honor of her amazing work as a scientist and inventor.

GREETINGS FROM THE FIRE-FREE **CUYAHOGA** RIVER!

Hi, Friend!

We're a little soggy from our underwater adventures, but we're still having fun. Maybe the most exciting—and hope-inspiring—thing about this part of our trip was visiting the Cuyahoga River. It's hard to believe it was so toxic that it used to catch fire on the regular. And now? Words can hardly describe how beautiful it is. And you know who's really happy about this change? Fish! At least we think they are happy—it's hard to tell. Do fish smile? Anyway, we're going for one more quick dip before we dry off and start exploring land.

Rock on!

Molly, Marc, and Sanden

Brains On! Buddy

Sitting with the Book

On Dry Land

(Probably)

PART 3
TOTALLY GROUNDED

LAND, SWEET LAND

Ah, land. It's home to some of our favorite things, like beaches, forests, mountains, and restaurants that give you free chips and salsa. There's so much to see! And a bonus: We can finally leave the ExPLORERR without being crushed, melted, smooshed, or drowned! We're about to pull up to the sandy shores of Lake Michigan. So let's lace up our shoes and get ready to walk and roll!

Whoa. Anyone else's legs feel like jelly?

I think all that time at sea messed with our sense of balance.

Yeah. Better take it slow as we check our supplies.

SNACKING LIST

- ☑ Oreo "dirt" pudding (with extra gummy worms!)
- ☑ *Sand*-wiches
- ☑ Ice pops
- ☑ Rock candy
- ☑ Peanuts in the shell (since the crust is like the earth's shell!)

PACKING LIST

- ☑ Sunblock (don't leave home without it—and we didn't!)
- ☑ Sandblock (to keep grains of sand from sticking to the sunblock you're wearing)
- ☑ Flip-flops and parkas (though not together, unless that's your style)
- ☑ Hoverboards (for when our feet get tired of walking)
- ☑ Personal water bottles and a water filtration and purification kit (in case we find some water and want to make it safe to drink)

ExPLORERR MaKEOVERR

- ✔ Windshield wipers (on every window!)

- ✔ Airless, puncture-resistant tires

- ✔ Camo Cover 3000, a shimmery coating that reflects our environment—from deserts to forests—so we don't scare the wildlife

- ✔ Vehicle-sized skis (way more fun than snow tires)

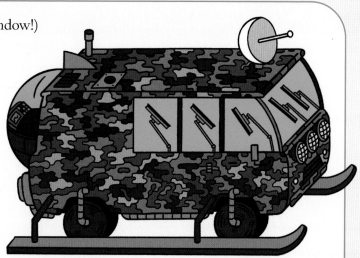

 **WARNING!** Just because we're out of the core *and* the water doesn't mean our adventure is suddenly safe. On land, we'll be facing dangerous caves and cliffs, bizarre rock formations, temperature extremes from the hottest deserts to the coldest glaciers...and *bears*! They look cuddly—but

SAND SMARTS

First stop: the beach! Some come for the water. Some come for the sun. We come for the sand! This stuff is amazing! Not only is it fun to squish between your toes, each grain also tells a story. So grab a shovel and pail, and let's dig into the science of sand!

Here's a question to keep you up at night: How many grains of sand do you think there are on planet Earth? A million? A billion? A *million billion*?! It would be impossible to scour every beach, desert, and riverbank to count them all, but through estimation, we have a rough number: approximately 7 quintillion, 500 quadrillion grains. Yes, that's a real number. Add the zeros and it looks like this: 7,500,000,000,000,000,000.

Phew. That's a *lot* of sand.

So where did it all come from?

Nope. Not the sand fairy. Sand comes from rocks!

Over many thousands—even millions—of years, as rivers have moved water to the oceans, they also have carried rocks in the flowing water. As those rocks are bumped and bounced around, they split into smaller and smaller pieces. When the rocks reach the ocean, the waves give them a good pounding too. Even weather can wear down stones over time. All that rough-and-tumble action means rocks break and break until, eventually, they

Oh, *not* the sand fairy? I'll just see myself out, then...

MYSTERY PHOTO

Focus your eyes on this mystery photo. Can you guess what it is? Turn to page 70 for the answer!

become those itsy-bitsy grains of sand we all know and love (unless they get stuck in our swimsuits). The most common rocks in sand are quartz, feldspar, and mica. But sand also has little pieces of shell and fish skeleton too! Sand is truly more than meets the eye.

PIT STOP

THE SINGING SANDS

Sand has incredible talents. And we're not just talking about its ability to stay in your hair days after you left the beach. Sand can also sing! Sort of. Sand dunes don't exactly yodel or belt out opera or anything like that. But they do make a very unusual, and very rare, noise. In fact, it's so rare that there are only thirty or forty places in the whole world where you can hear it. One of those places is the Great Sand Dunes National Park in Colorado. Imagine if a cello and an airplane had a baby, and that baby was yowling as loud as it could. The resulting noise would be a low, resonant, booming bellow. And that's pretty much what the singing sand dunes sound like.

Several important things have to happen just right to produce the otherworldly sounds of the singing sands. The grains of sand are all roughly the same size, which helps them roll over one another more easily. When an avalanche is triggered on the dune, the grains start sliding down, creating vibrations of sound that travel in waves through the dry layer of sand until they hit a hard, moist layer of sand that's almost like cement. The hard layer reflects the sound waves back, which then get trapped in the dry layer of sand, where the sound resonates. This creates that low, loud hum.

It doesn't happen every day. The conditions have to be just right. But when it does happen, the sound is unforgettable.

SAND COLORS

Did you know that sand comes in many different colors? Tour the world to see a rainbow of beaches!

TAN: This is by far the most common color of sand. You might think it's bland, but look closely and you can see lots of different shades and shapes.

WHITE: Snowy white beaches can be the product of quartz crystals or seashells, but in Hawaii, that white sand comes from parrotfish poop! They eat algae off coral. They digest the algae and poop out pristine white coral sand.

BLACK: A dark black beach is a beautiful sight to behold. That inky dark sand is made of volcanic material, including cooled lava and basalt rocks.

PINK: The pink sands located in Bermuda come from the breakdown of single-celled creatures called foraminifera. (Say that three times fast! Foraminifera, foraminifera, fora—oh, forget it!)

GREEN: These rare green sand beaches look kind of like they are covered in moss, but that grassy color comes from a mineral called olivine. There are only four of them known in the world.

We could party at the beach all day, but we've got a lot of ground to cover—literally. So let's swap our swim trunks for hiking shorts. We're heading into the forest to get the dirt on dirt!

THE DIRT ON SOIL

The forest is like a very quiet tea party. The birds chatter politely. The squirrels and raccoons listen in. The trees stand around awkwardly. It's peaceful, but we think the real action is underground. Dig down, and there's a whole secret world full of weird creatures, fascinating bacteria, cool roots, and lots of poop.

It's much easier to explore when you're super tiny, so we're going to break out our handy-dandy Zoom Ray and shrink down for this next leg of the journey. It's been a little glitchy lately, but we're sure it will work this time.

Let's see, this setting makes you grow. This one makes you float. This one makes you smell like cheese for some reason...

Here we go! Shrink Mode! Hold on to your hats! We're about to get microscopic!

PZZZAAAAAAMPHHH!

We did it! We shrank! And we smell only a little like cheese. We need to fix that later. For now, let's explore the amazing world of soil. Since we're even smaller than a grain of sand, we can clearly see all the different things in soil—and *wow*, there's a lot going on here.

First off, whatever you do, don't call soil *dirt*. It hates when you do that. Dirt refers to any old schmutz or grime. But soil is something very specific. It's made up of three distinct ingredients: sand, silt, and clay. These ingredients, in the right proportions, create soil that can nurture all sorts of plant life, from the veggies we eat to the trees that provide us with oxygen to breathe and shade on sunny days. Little critters also live in soil—from worms to bacteria. And it helps purify water. In short: Soil is special.

When you think about it, soil is like the earth's skin!

It's individual grains of sand! Each grain is as unique as a snowflake and as beautiful as a gem. They come from beaches all over the world and must be magnified 250 times before taking a photo like the one on page 67.

A grain of sand is incredibly tiny, but you can still see it without special equipment like a microscope (or Zoom Ray). Believe it or not, the grains of sand in soil are the biggest pieces in it! Particles of silt are much smaller. You'd need a magnifying glass to see them. Dry silt looks like cocoa powder—it's light, airy, and blows away very easily. *Whoosh!* If you mix silt with water, you'll get a very mushy form of mud. *Squish!*

Clay is the final ingredient in soil. Clay particles are teeny-tiny. When they're wet, they clump together. When they're dry, they're super-duper hard, almost like concrete. Clay is great for making pottery or sculptures—but pure clay can be really tough for plants to grow roots in. That's why good soil is a mixture of all three of these ingredients—and when they're found in equal parts, it's called loam. Loam is a practically perfect form of soil. Lots of different types of plants love to grow in loam. There's no place like loam!

While sand, silt, and clay are the main ingredients for soil, it can have lots of other things too. There are rocks, minerals, decomposing plant

MAKE YOUR HOME IN LOAM! CALL NOW FILLING UP FAST!

parts—even air and water! Soil is a whole world unto itself!

Plants + Soil = BFFs!

Shout-out to plants! They make our world a beautiful, shady, healthy, and even *delicious* place to live. They clean pollution out of the air and pump out oxygen for our lungs to breathe. They play an important role in the water cycle too. Plus, they are excellent listeners.

Just don't expect them to laugh at your jokes. They're a tough audience.

Like people, plants need air and water—and the soil is the number one delivery system for both! As plants stretch their roots into the soil, they find pockets of air. These pockets are small—unless you shrink down like us. At micro size, you can see that air makes up 20 to 30 percent of the soil around you. That's why giving plants too much water can be dangerous; flooding those pockets with water means the plants can't pull air from them. It's the plant version of drowning.

There's something else in soil that's very important to plants: nutrients. But—plot twist!—the plants can't access the nutrients without a little help from some special creatures.

Soil Party

Soil is the perfect home for about a bazillion organisms that make it better just by being there. It's like a big old party under our feet. Let's go mingle.

First, we've got bacteria. Bacteria might be the original party animals.

Recipe

Loam

INGREDIENTS:

- One part sand
- One part silt
- One part clay

DIRECTIONS:

Mix together all ingredients. Add a sprinkle of water and get ready to grow some happy plants! Makes a great base for mud pies!

After all, they're just about everywhere you look (we should say look with a microscope; they're so tiny you can't see them without one). They're joined by fungi and single-celled organisms called protozoa, along with nematodes too. And we can't forget soil's all-stars…worms! Worms are such heroes for the soil that some people keep a box of worms at home for their garden! They're not pets, exactly, but rather hard workers engaged in vermicomposting. That's when worms eat fruit and vegetable scraps, then break them down into castings (a fancy word for worm poop). Those castings can then be added to the soil. Plants love it!

BREAK IT DOWN
VERMICOMPOST

Vermi- = related to worms

-compost = make decayed matter into dirt

A Word About Worms

Waving at you, worms! As they wriggle through the soil, worms make little tunnels that allow water and oxygen to move into the soil—making it easier for plants to absorb those things through their roots. Not only that, worms have big appetites, and there are many delicious and delectable selections at the All-You-Can-Eat Soil Buffet—everything from bacteria to decomposing plant material. *Yum!*

The Poop Loop

So what are all these creatures doing in the dirt? Eating and pooping, basically. The party in the soil has a bit of a morbid side, because all those party-goers like to…eat one another. Generally speaking, eating your fellow guests is not good manners, but it's how these creatures survive.

One of the things that plants need most is an element called nitrogen. Sadly, plants can't just walk to the nitrogen store to get this stuff. First off, there is no nitrogen store. Second, plants can't walk. But lucky for them, there is a nitrogen delivery service… thanks to poop!

I have an order for a Ms. Connie Fur.

PLANT FOOD

Here's how it works: Let's say an animal is walking through the woods. Maybe a squirrel. Maybe a bear. When nature calls, the animal does its business right there in the dirt. Don't judge—they have to do it somewhere! This fresh poop delivery is chock-full of nitrogen. But plants can't simply eat the poop. It needs to be transformed first. Now guess what *can* and *will* eat that poop?

It's our little friends, the bacteria, fungi, and other organisms in the soil! They can't wait to chow down on a turd taco. *Nom nom nom!*

Then the really magical part happens (if eating poop can be considered magical). When the bacteria and fungi eat the poop, they convert the nitrogen in it to a water-soluble form. That's the form that plants need!

But wait! That's not all! Protozoa help too. They like to snack on bacteria burgers and fungi fajitas. When they chow down, they release the nitrogen from their meal into the soil. Then some microscopic worms called nematodes chomp up the protozoa…only to be eaten by some itsy-bitsy insects called arthropods. Everybody's eating, and everybody's pooping, and the soil is richer for it—full of essential nitrogen for plants. (Also, poop. It's full of poop. SO MUCH POOP. Just wanted to make that clear.)

We haven't given enough credit to the plants here, which bring their own super-powers to the soil. When a plant needs a certain type of mineral, such as phosphorus, it actually sends out signals through its roots. These signals are called exudate. If you think about a human sweating, that's similar to what the root does. The exudate is a sugary liquid that attracts just the right kind of organism to come closer and eat phosphorus in the soil. When that organism poops the phosphorus out in a water-soluble form, the plant's roots can absorb it. This cool system of signals is how plants can make sure they get just what they need—all thanks to their sweetly sweating roots!

No fair! All I get from my sweat are pit stains.

FANTASTIC FORMATIONS

Our tour of the soil was fun, but we'd better un-shrink soon…before some hungry insect eats us and we end up part of the poop loop! Let's just reset the Zoom Ray (*click, click, click*) and zap ourselves back to normal size!

ZHWUH-VOOOOOOM! Ah, much better. So long, soil friends! Time to hop back in the ExPLORERR and travel on! Also, does anyone else have a strong cheese craving?

CALLING ALL CANYONS

Canyons are the supermodels of geography. They've got stunning, steep walls and incredible views. They look great in every season, and they're always gorgeous in photos. No worldwide road trip would be complete without visiting a few of these natural wonders.

The word "canyon" comes from the Spanish *cañón*, which means "tube." A canyon has steep, rocky sides with a valley down below. Canyons can be found on every continent except Antarctica. There are even underwater ones that are called submarine canyons! The Grand Canyon in the United States is one of the most famous canyons in the world.

Take this, and if a canyon doesn't form in a few million years, give me a call.

Canyons can form in different ways, but scientists generally agree that two important elements are required: water and time.

A river, for example, flows over the ground and carries away little bits of rock and soil as it goes. The longer it does this, the more land it carries away—until eventually, the river carves a deep ditch. If this goes on for millions of years, a mighty canyon is made!

Weather and erosion can help build canyons too. Water that gets trapped in a small crack on a rock can freeze in cold weather. Since frozen water expands (to find out why, see page 51), it can make the crack bigger—and even split the rock in half! Over time, more and more rocks are damaged by this process. As they break into pieces, some of the broken rocks tumble downhill to lower ground. Heavy rains can help the process along. Eventually, this makes a wider and wider opening between two cliffs. The result is, you guessed it, a canyon!

Canyons aren't just gorgeous geographic wonders. Scientists study them to uncover clues about how the earth formed and what changes have happened to our planet over time. There are lots of well-preserved fossils in canyons that tell

GRAND CANYON SCAVENGER HUNT

If you visit the Grand Canyon, you might see

- Fossils

- Tusayan Ruin, where Pueblo people lived 800 years ago

- Ponderosa pine forests

- Wildlife like coyotes, bighorn sheep, and rattlesnakes (just remember, no feeding the animals!)

- Endangered species like the California condor

- Tourists (it's okay to feed the tourists, but you should probably ask first or it might get weird)

us about ancient creatures. Entire civilizations, such as the Hopi people, have built homes and communities along the steep sides of canyons. Hundreds of different species of wildlife can be found living in canyons too. It's no wonder canyons have so many fans!

I'm the president of my local canyon fan club. Our motto is "Yes, we can-yon!"

Types of Canyons

- **River canyons** are formed by the slow and steady flow of water on rocks. Over time—millions of years or more—the water erodes the rocks, cutting a channel through them until a canyon is formed. You will often find a river still flowing through the bottom of a canyon.

- **Slot canyons** form when weathering and erosion affect softer rocks, like sandstone. Slot canyons tend to have very narrow openings at the top—and are dangerously deep. If you ever find yourself near a slot canyon, be *extra* careful!

- **Box canyons** have an opening at only one end. They are the dead-end roads of canyons. They are made of harder rock than slot canyons.

BRAVE THE CAVE

Fire up the headlights! We're exploring cave country next! Caves are naturally occurring openings in rock or earth, which means they aren't made by humans, as mines are. They are usually dark and quiet, making them the perfect place to go when you want to get away from it all.

Caves are found worldwide, and they come in many shapes and sizes. As long as it's big enough to hold a human, it's considered a cave. There are caves made of limestone where you can find dramatic stalactites dripping from the roof. There are caves inside icy glaciers that gleam green and blue. There are even caves near volcanoes that contain tubes or tunnels left behind from lava flow.

Want to go a little deeper? Let's hop out of the ExPLORERR and see what we find. Don't forget your headlamp! One thing all caves have in common is complete and total darkness. Imagine the darkest night without the moon or any stars.

Caves are even darker than that.

SUPER COOL SCIENTIST

MARC OHMS

If you like exploring small (or ginormous), dark places where no one has ever been before, Marc Ohms has your dream job: He's a physical science technician at Wind Cave National Park in the Black Hills of South Dakota.

In 2004, Marc began searching for a "back door" entrance to Wind Cave. He found a new hole that was moving airflow—a good sign that there's a cave passage lurking behind it—but there were a couple of problems. First, it was too small for him to fit through. Second, it was jam-packed with *rattlesnakes*! After the rattlesnakes left, Marc began the long, slow process of enlarging the hole so he could fit inside. It's taken Marc more than a decade to descend about 200 feet in the new cave. Since he was the one to discover it, he got to name it—and he chose the perfect name for a cave that has been so hard to explore: Persistence Cave. Marc hopes that one day he'll be able to prove that Persistence Cave connects to Wind Cave.

FACT-ASTIC VOYAGE

Stalactite or stalagmite? It's easy to get these two terms confused. A *stalactite* happens when water drips down from the roof of a cave, bringing minerals with it, creating a rock formation that looks like a jagged icicle. A *stalagmite*, on the other hand, happens when water drips from the cave roof onto the cave floor, eventually building up into a rock formation.

You can remember which is which this way: Ceiling starts with C, so you can find stalaCtites there. And ground starts with G, so that's where the stalaGmites are!

Most caves are made of limestone or other rocks that can dissolve from the slow and steady flow of carbonic acid. The cavern fills up with carbonic acid, which slowly dissolves the ceiling, walls, and floors.

Wait, acid? *Ahhh! Run for your life!*

Just kidding! It's not as dangerous as it sounds. Carbonic acid is the same stuff in soda that makes your mouth tingle when you drink it. Carbonic acid is a very weak acid, which is why it takes such a long time for caves to form—millions of years or more!

At first glance, you might not think much of a cave, but there is so much happening and so much that *has* happened in these wondrous formations. For example, take a look at the walls of Spain's Altamira cave. The images of bison date back over 15,000 years, and they show not only that our ancestors hunted these animals but also how important they were to human survival. These days you might get in trouble for drawing on the walls of your home, but back then it would have been a prized part of your cave dwelling.

Humans aren't the only ones who found a home in caves. From one-of-a-kind

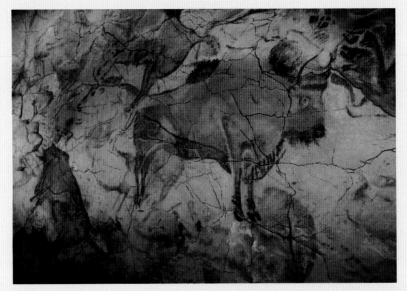

microbes to spiders with no eyes, creatures of all shapes and sizes have adapted to live and thrive in darkness. Take our mammalian cousin the bat! There are over 1,300 different species of these upside-down-sleeping flying mammals, and the majority like to make their homes in caves. Oh, and watch your step. *There's gold in them thar caves.* Actually, it's bat poop—or as it's usually called, guano—but it is definitely valuable. The floors of some caves are covered in bat guano, which is highly valued as a natural fertilizer. You know what they say: One animal's turd is another animal's treasure!

Road Trip SOUVENIR

PET ROCK

Meet our newest BFF—our very own Pet Rock! We named it Hubert. Hubert is from the Grand Canyon. We suspect that Hubert is a piece of cliff called the Redwall Limestone—it's actually gray, but it has turned reddish from iron staining. When we get it under a microscope, we might even find a fossil or two from when this part of the Grand Canyon was underwater, 340 million years ago.

There's a lot you can learn from rocks, and studying them is a key part of geology. We got permission to study this rock in the lab back at Headquarters, but you should always leave rocks, and other objects from nature, where you found them. In the Grand Canyon, it's illegal to take rocks without permission. Rock on, rocks!

WEIRD ROCKS

There are strange, unusual, and even astonishing rock formations all around the world. Here are a few of our favorites!

Giant's Causeway, Northern Ireland

More than 40,000 columns made of black basalt rock extend into the Atlantic Ocean at Giant's Causeway. Most of them are shaped like hexagons! That means they have six sides! These cool shapes were formed by lava

seeping through the earth's crust. According to legend, a giant created this rocky path to travel from Northern Ireland to Scotland.

Death Valley's sailing stones, United States

One of the hottest, driest spots on earth, Death Valley also contains a strange mystery. In a section of Death Valley called Racetrack Playa, rocks seem to slide across the dry, rocky ground—all by themselves! No one has ever *seen* the rocks move, but their movement leaves long trails behind them. It's a strange sight! Scientists think the movement is caused by winter winds that push the rocks on thin chunks of ice.

Mount Erebus, Antarctica

The combination of hot steam from this active volcano and frigid temperatures results in hollow ice towers that can be more than thirty feet tall! It would be a great place to visit if it weren't (a) far away, (b) freezing cold, and (c) an active volcano.

Cave of the Crystals, Mexico

The world's largest crystals are hidden in this stunning but dangerous cave. One crystal is thirty-nine feet long—about the length of a school bus! We can thank the power of magma for creating this wonder under the Sierra de Naica, a mountain that's rich in silver, gold, lead, and zinc. It's so hot and damp in the Cave of the Crystals, though, that scientists must wear special cooling suits to study it for short periods of time.

MEGA MATCHUP
MOUNT EVEREST VS. GRAND CANYON

Who's ready for a fight to the finish between two rocky marvels? In one corner, Mount Everest, the tallest point on the entire planet. And in the other corner, the Grand Canyon, one of the most famous canyons in the world. Both made the cut on the list of the Seven Natural Wonders of the World, so prepare yourself for an especially fierce face-off!

TEAM MOUNT EVEREST

- At its peak, Mount Everest stands more than 29,000 feet above sea level. Mount Everest isn't content to hold the record for highest point on planet Earth, though. It keeps growing, getting taller by a quarter inch every year!

- Climbing Mount Everest is literally breathtaking—the atmosphere is so thin up there that hikers must carry their own oxygen tanks to survive the trek.

- Reaching the summit, or top, of Mount Everest is the ultimate physical and mental test for humans. It takes *at least* a year of training to build up your physical strength, cardiovascular system, and tolerance of high altitudes.

- Mount Everest is all about extremes, from subzero temps to winds that top one hundred miles per hour. No wonder it's extremely awesome too!

- Incredible (and rare) creatures like snow leopards, red pandas, and Himalayan black bears all live on Mount Everest.

TEAM GRAND CANYON

- The Grand Canyon, which is 1 mile deep, is 277 miles long and as much as 18 miles wide in some places, with a total of 1,904 square miles—making it bigger than the state of Rhode Island!

- The Grand Canyon is one of the most popular national parks in the United States, with around 6 million visitors every year.

- Entering the Grand Canyon is like reserving a seat in nature's time machine. You'll see fossils everywhere—if you keep your eyes open! Watch for 270-million-year-old fossils of sea creatures from the Permian period...and fossilized footprints from long-extinct reptiles...and even 506-million-year-old trilobites that once cruised the ocean floor like ancient Roombas.

- Love animals? Then the Grand Canyon is the destination vacation for you! More than ninety species of mammals and forty-seven species of reptiles call the Grand Canyon home. You might spot bats, bison, hogs, mountain lions—or even an elk or a super rare California condor!

- Ever wondered what's at the very bottom of the Grand Canyon? Oh, it's just some 2-billion-year-old rocks...and the Colorado River, which made the Grand Canyon possible!

Which rock formation is cooler: Mount Everest or Grand Canyon?

YOUR VERDICT

HIGH AND DRY IN THE DESERT

We're back in the ExPLORERR, and we're cruising through the desert at sixty-five miles per hour! Oh, wait, now it's fifty-five…now it's thirty-five…now it's five…and now we've stopped. What's going on? Is the hood supposed to smoke like that? Did the engine always sound like an angry moose? Better take a look before we move on.

Lucky for us, walking might be the best way to experience the desert. If you drive by too quickly, you might think deserts are nothing but dry, empty wastelands. If you stop and look closely, though, you'll see all kinds of remarkable plants and animals living there. Plus, there are stunning land formations and some of the best sunsets on earth.

Deserts are places of extremes. While they can be super hot during the daytime, some get really cold at night, with temperatures plunging to freezing or below.

In fact, there are several different types of desert. But they all have one thing in common: Deserts are dry, dry, dry places where there's very little water or precipitation. So before we go any farther, go ahead and grab a tall glass of water. Just reading about deserts can make you thirsty!

Types of Deserts

Around the globe, there are four main types of deserts:

- **Arid deserts** are probably what most people think of when they hear the word "desert." These deserts are hot and dry almost year-round, though temperatures at night can get very chilly. Winter brings small amounts of rain—as little as a half inch or so. The Sahara in Africa is a famous arid desert.

- **Semiarid deserts** are less hot than arid deserts. Their highest temp is around 100 degrees Fahrenheit, while arid deserts can reach 120 degrees Fahrenheit and higher! In the winter, semiarid deserts get more rain too. You can find these deserts in states like Utah, Nevada, and Montana.

- **Coastal deserts**, like the Atacama Desert in Chile, are created when cold winds from the ocean blow over land. The cold air can't hold moisture, so there's less precipitation. These winds can bring fog, so coastal deserts can feel damp even though they get very little rain. The temperatures aren't as extreme as other deserts, but some coastal deserts have gone decades without a single drop of rain.

- **Cold deserts** tend to have longer, colder winters—and they can get a lot of snow too! Nearly the entire continent of Antarctica is known as a **polar desert**. There's a lot of water trapped in the ice, but since it's not available to plants or animals, the area is considered a desert.

A Land of Sand

As you know, we're sand fans. And deserts have lots of the stuff. But how? They're not near beaches, lakes, or rivers. Beach sand, you'll remember, is the result of rocks that have been broken into minuscule pieces thanks to the power of water. Some of the desert sand has been through the same process, but it happened long ago, when the area was wetter—before it became a desert. Desert sand also comes from the slow and steady erosion of rocks over time.

There's another origin for desert sand. Remember how soil contains a mixture of sand, silt, and clay? In a hot, dry desert, there often aren't many plants that can use their roots to help keep the soil in place. As a result, wind can blow away the lightweight particles of silt and dry clay—leaving behind only sand.

Sand dunes in the desert are formed by wind. Even a gentle breeze can pick up grains of sand, swirling them around in the air before depositing them into mounds of different heights. Watch out for strong winds in the desert—they can cause a sandstorm!

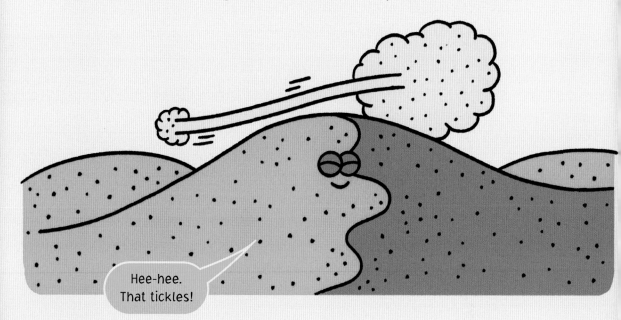

Chill Out

So how do animals survive in the extreme conditions of deserts? They have come up with some pretty clever tricks! Many desert animals are active only at dawn, dusk, or night, when it's cooler. They avoid the high heat of full sun. Animals can also seek out spots that are not quite so hot, such as the shade cast by a cactus or a large rock. Small mammals dig burrows, since the temperature is cooler underground without the full force of the sun.

TOP WAYS TO STAY COOL (WITH A LITTLE HELP FROM THE ANIMAL KINGDOM)

If the heat's got you beat, take a tip from these desert dwellers!

- Grow extra-long ears like jackrabbits to help your body shed extra heat.

- Sleep through the heat, like round-tailed ground squirrels.

- Hide underground, like desert toads. Then, when it rains, hop to the surface and splash in the puddles!

- Pee on your own legs, like vultures—as long as you don't mind losing all your friends!

Or you can grab a Popsicle and hop in a pool! No pee necessary!

Water Work-Arounds

We know water is a necessary component for almost all living things, yet those that live in the desert have come up with some amazing adaptations to thrive even with very little of the wet stuff. Here's how they do it:

- **Big stems:** Cacti have enlarged stems for storing more water than most plants. Their sharp spines help them protect their water stash too—stay away, thirsty critters, or get poked!

- **Slurping sap:** Animals often find ways around a plant's defenses to get at juicy leaves, sap, and fruit. These plant parts can be full of water to help an animal hydrate.

- **Bug bites:** Some animals can get enough fluids from eating bugs—and the desert has a *lot* of insects, so there's plenty for everyone that wants some!

- **Kidney power:** Some desert rodents have special kidneys that make sure their bodies hold on to as much water as possible.

- **Water wizards:** Amazingly, kangaroo rats have figured out how to get enough water from seeds. They won't drink water even if you give it to them!

FACT-ASTIC VOYAGE

An oasis is an area within a desert that has a supply of fresh water. Sometimes the water comes from springs or an underground reservoir called an aquifer. Generally, an oasis has enough water that plants, food crops, and even trees like palm or date trees can grow there, despite the dry climate.

DESERT DWELLERS

Let's hear a cheer for creatures that brave extreme temps and dryness to call the desert home! Surviving the epic heat isn't their only superpower.

- The black-tailed jackrabbit has enormous black-tipped ears and, naturally, a black tail. It can reach speeds of forty miles per hour when it runs!

- The kangaroo rat is a small rodent with long, strong back feet. It can jump nine feet in a single bound to escape predators!

- Coyotes, which are related to dogs, have long, narrow faces and bushy tails. They can eat almost anything—from bugs and rodents to fruit and grass.

- The deadly rattlesnake has a diamond-shaped head and is usually two to four feet long. Their telltale rattle is made of keratin—the same stuff your fingernails are made of! Watch out—they are very poisonous.

- New World vultures, which are found in North America, South America, and Central America, have a wide wingspan for gliding and a hooked beak for ripping up carcasses. Their bald heads let them eat rotting meat without their feathers getting infected by bacteria.

- Gila monsters are a type of large, venomous lizard. Their bites are extremely painful because they chomp down repeatedly to send venom through grooves in their teeth. So if you see one coming, head the other way.

ALL-STAR ANIMAL NAVIGATORS

GLACIER GREATNESS

After our unexpected desert detour, we need to cool off. And there's no better place to chill out than on ice caps and glaciers. After all, almost 10 percent of the earth's land is covered in ice. Let's bundle up and skate on over to check out these frozen wonders.

Since the earth still has ice sheets on it, we're technically in an ice age...which is a pretty *cool* fact, am I right?

The most massive glacier on the planet began as a single snowflake. Glaciers are formed when, over many years, lots of snow is compacted down into a thick mass of ice. What makes them really unique is that glaciers are able to flow, which means they don't sit still. The combination of their own weight plus gravity makes glaciers move slowly. And like slow-motion bulldozers, they can move soil and rocks, reshaping the landscape along the way.

Glaciers are also super important to the water cycle. More than 68 percent of the entire planet's supply of fresh water is locked within glacial ice. During winter, glaciers tend to get bigger, while in summer, they shrink as they partially melt from the warmth of the sun. That partial melting means that valuable fresh water enters the water cycle again, even replenishing rivers that began to dry up in the summer heat.

On Thin Ice

If all of the earth's ice melted, our planet would be unrecognizable. The oceans would rise by more than 200 feet, and coastal cities would vanish underwater. It's not a pretty thought.

Glaciers and ice caps go through a cycle of freezing, melting, and then refreezing. They've done that for thousands of years. While it's normal for glaciers to change size from season to season, glaciers and ice caps are now melting at an alarming rate, thanks to climate change. Climate change describes many ways in which the planet's climate is altered over time, while global warming specifically refers to how the planet is getting warmer. It's getting warmer because of us. Humans are burning oil and other fossil fuels and releasing gases into the air that over time trap more and more heat. It's like throwing more and more invisible blankets over the earth, making it quite toasty. Because of that increase in temperature, glaciers are melting faster than they can refreeze.

People have been photographing the natural world for almost 200 years—and the historical photos of glaciers from decades ago have captured a dramatic and devastating transformation. The photographic proof that glaciers are disappearing is undeniable. The collapse of glaciers can lead to disasters like flooding and avalanches, in addition to rising sea levels. Scientists all over the world are working together to

find ways to slow climate change and protect our planet.

Satellites in space can take pictures of glaciers so scientists can see how fast they are shrinking. More scientists than ever are studying this phenomenon and telling the world how urgently we need to protect the glaciers by combating climate change—before they disappear forever.

Glacier Groupies

At first glance, glaciers might look like frozen, deserted wastelands where no life-forms could survive, but take a closer look and you'll find that the opposite is true. Large animals with heavy coats—like bison, reindeer, and elk—head to the glaciers for relief from summer heat. They sprawl out on the ice to chill out! Sometimes they find pockets of cold air that blow off the glaciers. It's like their own personal air conditioner.

Nineteen types of birds can be found on glaciers, including golden eagles, ravens, and snow buntings. Most birds that visit the glaciers are searching for food. For a long time, scientists believed that penguins were the only birds to nest on the ice—until it was discovered that the white-winged diuca finch brings twigs and grasses to construct nests high on icy cliffsides.

Even though glaciers can be bitterly cold, that doesn't stop bugs from living there. Glacial midges, ice worms, snow fleas, and other insects can all be found on glaciers. So believe it or not, many creatures think life on ice is very nice!

Hi, Friend!

Wow! What a wonderful, weird, and wild world we live in. From sand to soil, canyon to mountain, desert to ice cap…there's something here for everyone. One thing is for sure: This land has been around for a long, long time, and there's always more to explore. By the way, if you are exploring, be sure to bring a map and compass—or at least a lot of peanut shells to mark your trail!

We're not sure if anything in the sky can compete with the diversity and grandeur of the earth, but we're about to find out as we get ready to soar into the wild blue yonder. Up, up, and away!

With our heads in the clouds,

Molly, Marc, and Sanden

Our Pal

Next to the Sand Castle

By the Folding Chair

Under the Umbrella

PART 4
SKY'S THE LIMIT

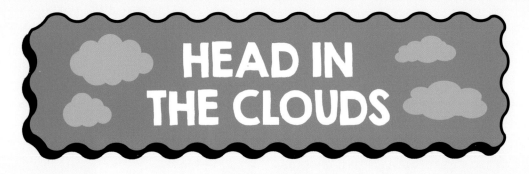

HEAD IN THE CLOUDS

3...2...1...LIFTOFF! We're getting in touch with our inner airheads as we leave the earth's surface and explore the sky—and beyond! What's up? We are!

Welcome to ExPLORERR Airways! Where you can fly like a bird without having to eat like one! Have some snacks!

SNACKING LIST

Obviously, we need some out-of-this-world treats at the ready before we go seriously off-road.

- ☑ Sunflower seeds
- ☑ MoonPies
- ☑ Cotton candy (a sweet reminder of puffy clouds)
- ☑ Snow cones
- ☑ Rocket Pops

PACKING LIST

- ☑ Sunblock
- ☑ Oxygen tanks
- ☑ Personal jet packs
- ☑ Barf bags (just hope we won't need these!)
- ☑ Parachutes (in case rough winds cause an air emergency!)
- ☑ Gel, comb, and blow-dryer (in case rough winds cause a hair emergency!)

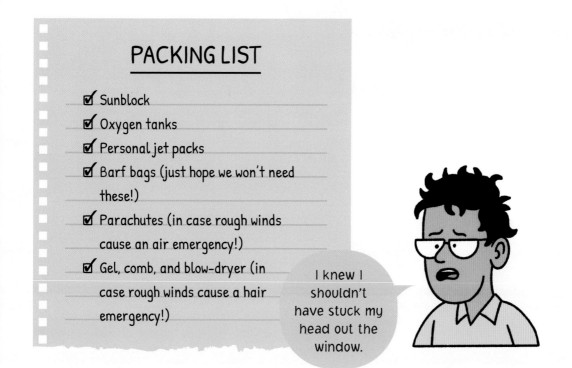

I knew I shouldn't have stuck my head out the window.

ExPLORERR MaKEOVERR

Time to break out all the awesome flight and weather-forecasting gear we've collected over the years. Today's forecast calls for a 100 percent chance of cool gadgets.

ADDING

- ✔ Weather station
- ✔ Wings
- ✔ Jet propulsion engine
- ✔ Cabin pressurization system
- ✔ Solar panels
- ✔ A birdhouse

WARNING!

We're going up into the wild blue yonder—and we mean *wild*. Our travel forecast includes everything from bumpy turbulence (buckle up!) to surprise storms to lower-than-normal oxygen levels. Not to mention the chance of lightning, meteorites, and radiation from the sun! And to top it all off, this flight has no Wi-Fi! But we doubt you'll notice with all the sightseeing we've got planned.

THE DELICIOUS LAYERS OF THE
ATMOSPHERE

Just like the ocean and earth, the atmosphere—the air that circulates around our planet—contains different layers. If your brain works like ours, then it probably helps to picture this in terms of food. So imagine the sky like a massive, floating, five-layer bean dip. Let's explore layer by layer.

TROPOSPHERE

This is the lowest layer of our atmosphere (aka the refried beans), and it reaches about six miles above the earth's surface on average. This layer contains the air we breathe—and it's where almost all weather happens! Thankfully, there aren't actually beans up here, so we never have to deal with pinto storms or bean-nadoes.

STRATOSPHERE

Above the troposphere is the stratosphere (aka the guacamole). The stratosphere is above the clouds, and it's where the essential ozone layer is located (more on that on page 119). And like guacamole, it's smooth. That's why planes fly in the stratosphere—it helps them avoid turbulence. The stratosphere starts at the edge of the troposphere and reaches thirty-one miles above the ground.

Pass the chips!

MESOSPHERE

Next up is the mesosphere (aka the sour cream). It's a cold layer of the atmosphere where the air is too thin for people to breathe. The mesosphere is where most meteors burn up as they zoom toward the earth. We're guessing that a giant field of sour cream straight out of the fridge could extinguish a few meteors too. The upper edge of the mesosphere is fifty-three miles above the earth.

THERMOSPHERE

Higher and higher we zoom until we reach the thermosphere (aka the salsa). This layer of the atmosphere absorbs intense ultraviolet (UV) radiation and X-rays from the sun. Those rays increase the temperature to a whopping 900 to 3,500 degrees Fahrenheit or higher—now, that's some spicy salsa! The thermosphere is also where you can find satellites orbiting the earth and where the aurora puts on a breathtaking light show. The thermosphere is at least 300 miles above the earth.

EXOSPHERE

Kind of like gooey, melting cheese, this layer has no clearly defined boundary with space, and to make matters even more strange, it appears that the air is so thin in the exosphere that the earth's atmosphere is gradually slipping through it into space! Luckily, gravity keeps most of our atmosphere right where it belongs. This tortilla chip will put our five-layer bean dip where *it* belongs: in our mouths! *CHOMP!*

THE AIR UP THERE

The expression "head in the clouds" can mean you're not paying attention to what's going on around you. But for this trip, we want our heads in the clouds! As we zoom into the atmosphere, we're going to get up close and personal with clouds, wind, and whatever weather we encounter.

Whoosh! The wind in the troposphere is what keeps kites flying high. It's what makes trees sway back and forth. And it fills the sails of ships. We can't see it, but we can feel its power, like when it pushes against the ExPLORERR. Naturally, we have the latest and greatest technology to help our wings adjust, so the blowing winds don't send us off course. We want to know more about this invisible wonder, so we're going to ride the breeze and see where it takes us.

The easiest way to understand wind is that it's simply air moving from one place to another. Air is made up of different gases, and those gases have mass. When you feel a gentle breeze on your face, you're actually feeling the mass of the gases in the wind. But the amount of air in our atmosphere is *way* more than you'll find in a gentle breeze. Air can push down on us with a powerful amount of pressure at the lower points on our planet, like at sea level.

Highs and Lows

So why is air always rushing around anyway? Is it late for a tea party? Is it training for a marathon? Did it drink too much soda and now it just can't sit still? It turns out that air moves and wind blows in large part thanks to heat from the sun.

You see, air likes to move from areas where there is lots of air to areas where there is less air. It's like if you had an empty bathtub and poured all the water into the left side. That water wouldn't just sit there—it would rush to the area with no water to even things out. That's what air does too. But unlike a bathtub, the amount of air on the surface of the earth is always changing due to heat from the sun. This means air has to constantly rush around to balance things out.

It works like this: When the sun heats up a spot on earth, the air there gets warm. Warm air expands and rises. As that air floats up, up, up—like so many tiny, invisible balloons—there is suddenly less air near the ground. Less air = less pressure from air pushing on you. So, naturally, we call this an area with *low pressure*.

When a spot on earth is cooler, the air does the opposite: It gets denser and sinks down, down, down. This means there is suddenly a lot more air around you, a *higher* amount. We call this a *high-pressure* zone. Like that water in the bathtub, air wants to go from places with a *high* amount of air to places with a *low* amount of air. As it zooms from a high-pressure area to a low-pressure one, it creates wind!

Another way to make wind...eat a bunch of beans! *Toot toot!*

Wind blows more easily when there are fewer things in the way. If an area has lots of trees, for example, the trees will disrupt the wind and slow it down. Mountains can also impact the way wind blows. Large areas of water are generally open and flat, but as the wind gets faster it whips up the waves, making them stronger. Then the waves can disrupt the wind too.

Next time you feel a breeze, remember it's just air rushing around trying to balance things out here on earth. It's a big job, so no wonder air is under so much pressure!

I like to give air plenty of encouragement by shouting things like "Way to blow!" and "Wind for the win!"

HIGH FIVE, O_2!

One of the best things about living on earth is all the oxygen. We already know how important oxygen atoms are in water—one oxygen atom and two hydrogen atoms make up every molecule of water in the universe. And check this out: If you have *two* oxygen atoms together, they form a molecule of oxygen gas (or O_2). O_2 is oh so important for our health. We can't live without it! So let's spend some quality time with our GFF (gas friend forever). To start, why not suck millions of O_2 molecules into your lungs as you take a big, deep breath. Ahhhh. Doesn't friendship feel great?

Oxygen is great at making lots of friends, actually. By that we mean it loves bonding with other elements. And it likes to travel the whole world too, which it does by riding the wind into the higher regions of our atmosphere. It can even race around the world on a jet stream—that's like a river of air flowing through our atmosphere! Many miles high in our atmosphere, the jet stream sends weather systems around the world…and oxygen too!

FACT-ASTIC VOYAGE

Long ago, the earth's atmosphere was *very* different. It was mostly made up of ammonia, methane, neon, and water vapor—which would have made it impossible for us to breathe! Then early, single-celled life-forms began to produce oxygen, which, over eons, built up in our atmosphere. Thanks, little dudes!

Interestingly, the air we breathe is not 100 percent oxygen—not even close. Only about 21 percent of the atmosphere is oxygen gas. Nitrogen gas makes up an astonishing 78 percent of the atmosphere. That last 1 percent is a mixture of small amounts of many gases, including hydrogen and carbon dioxide. That magic mixture of gases is pretty standard on earth—as long as you stay close to the ground. If you climb to the top of a mountain, there's less air around you. Because the air is thin, it has fewer oxygen molecules for you to breathe.

WEATHER PATTERNS

An important part of weather forecasting is figuring out the relationship between cold, dry areas of air and warm, moist areas of air. Think of it like an invisible wrestling match happening in the sky. Cold air has a signature move to overtake an area of warm air: It's called a cold front. Ah, but warm air has a signature move of its own: It's called the cranberry belly flop! Just kidding. When warm air overtakes cold air, it's called a warm front.

Winds, including jet streams, help move cold and warm fronts across the planet. We definitely need to pay attention to when weather fronts happen, because when two different air masses clash, they can cause turbulence. And that, friends, can lead to storms! It's the weather equivalent of a body slam!

Cold fronts move faster than warm fronts and can bring dramatic weather changes like big storms. Since cold fronts have heavier air, they push warm fronts up above them, where the warm, wet air can form new cloud systems, and even thunderstorms—*kaboom!*

When a warm front comes in, it moves more slowly because it's difficult to push the heavier cold front out of the way. Instead, the warm front moves over it, creating storms in the troposphere. It's an epic sky-side smackdown, and you can watch it every night by tuning in to your local weather forecast!

WEATHER GONE WILD

Extreme weather is extremely dangerous…but also extremely interesting! We're going to (carefully) pilot the ExPLORERR near some storms to learn more. We can't promise a smooth ride, but we *can* promise amazing facts.

As we fly over warm ocean waters, we can see a hurricane brewing. Let's get a closer look. Also known as a tropical cyclone, a hurricane can occur when warm, wet air rises off the surface of the ocean and creates a pocket of low pressure below. Then higher-pressure air rushes into the pocket, gets warmed by the ocean, and starts to rise too. The result is a swirling, whirling storm that can get more dangerous—even deadly—as it grows.

A tropical cyclone doesn't become a hurricane until its winds reach 74 miles per hour. After that, hurricanes fall into five categories, depending on their wind speed. Hurricane season lasts from June through November each year. That's when hurricanes are most likely to make landfall. Even though hurricanes weaken over land, they can still do tremendous damage before they fade away.

Don't think you can escape severe storms just by traveling inland. While hurricanes aren't as big of an issue there, you'll need to watch out for tornadoes. A tornado is like a vertical tube of high-speed wind that stretches from a thunderstorm to the ground. Because wind is invisible, so are tornadoes—until they pick up debris or rain!

FACT-ASTIC VOYAGE

The United States has more tornadoes than any other country in the world—more than 1,000 each year.

Lightning, ferocious winds, and hail as big as your fist make tornadoes devastating, and sometimes deadly, weather events. Tornadoes form when cold, dry air crashes into warm, wet air. The sun has a role to play too: heating the ground and the atmosphere to provide the warm air. That's why tornadoes are more likely to form in the afternoon—but they can happen at any time. They can pop up quickly too, which is why meteorologists—that's the name for scientists who predict the weather—take tornadoes so seriously. A tornado watch means that the conditions are right for a tornado to form. A tornado warning means that a tornado has been spotted by weather watchers (or has appeared on radar) and that anyone in the area should take shelter immediately.

Whoa! Looks like we got a little *too* close! Our van is getting batted around by air currents like a piñata at a party! Time to scram from this storm…before we're scrambled ourselves!

TOOLS OF THE TRADE

Every fortune-teller has a favorite tool. For some, it's a crystal ball. Others like to read tea leaves.

Meteorologists use a whole bunch of things to predict the weather. One tool is called an anemometer. It's an instrument that measures the speed of wind. Another is radar, which tracks how wind is moving within clouds. It does this by sending bursts of microwaves from a transmitter. It won't work if the sky is clear, since the radar beams need something to bounce off. Clouds are chock-full of tiny particles that are just perfect for that, like raindrops or snowflakes. Radar also works if there's a lot of dust in the air—or even a lot of bugs or birds!

Thermometers and barometers are powerhouses of weather prediction. Thermometers are used to measure air temperature. Barometers measure atmospheric (or air) pressure. In other words, a barometer tells us how much the air is pushing down on us. By measuring changes in temperature and atmospheric pressure, we can figure out which areas have high air pressure and which areas have low pressure. As we learned earlier, wind likes to move from high-pressure zones to low-pressure ones, so we use these two tools to get a good idea of what weather is on the way—including when a storm is brewing.

BREAK IT DOWN
METEOROLOGY

Meteor- = from the Greek wor
meaning "of the atmospher

-ology = the study of

MYSTERY PHOTO

Focus your eyes on this mystery photo. Can you guess what it is? Turn to the next page for the answer!

Here are some other tools scientists use to predict the weather:

- **Rain gauge:** This measures the amount of rain that has fallen.

- **Satellite:** This orbits the earth about 22,000 miles above us to take pictures of weather systems.

- **Weather balloon:** These enormous balloons are released every twelve hours, all over the world. They are attached to special boxes that collect data from the atmosphere every second and transmit information about the temperature, wind speed and direction, humidity, and air pressure.

- **Supercomputer:** This runs complicated math equations to analyze lots of data sets. It would take a person years to solve the kind of math that supercomputers can complete in a few seconds. Entering data—about past storms and present conditions—and running that through complex equations let supercomputers predict the weather.

All this technology means that weather forecasts are generally about 90 percent accurate for the next five days. After that, the accuracy tends to drop. There are simply too many variables at play. That's when weather forecasters must make educated guesses—there's no surefire way to know exactly, with 100 percent certainty, what the weather will be. It's unpredictable—to say the least! Some people say that weather forecasting is more like a technical art than a science, but meteorologists do their best. As scientists continue to improve weather-forecasting technology, our weather forecasts get more and more accurate.

I can't predict the weather, but I can predict you'll turn the page in 3...2...1...

ANSWER!

It's a weather balloon! While you won't find this type of balloon at a birthday party, it's an important tool to help us monitor the weather. Weather balloons are launched twice a day from more than 900 different places around the globe. Weather balloons each carry a special passenger, a device called a radiosonde. As it rises into the atmosphere, the radiosonde measures air pressure, temperature, and humidity.

SNOW WONDER

Snow can mean a day off from school…a fun time sledding…or a take-no-prisoners snowball fight! There's nothing in nature quite so enchanting as a quiet snowfall on a cold winter's night. And there's nothing quite as annoying as having to shovel the walkway when it's freezing cold out. It takes millions of snowflakes to make a snowstorm—and guess what? The rumors are true: No two snowflakes are alike! But how is that even possible?

All snowflakes start out the same way—as a water droplet in a cloud. Clouds are mostly made of many water droplets, even when the temperature is below freezing. As the temperature continues to fall, though, the droplets start to freeze. And that's when the magic happens: The droplets don't all freeze at once. Instead, they freeze one at a time. As each water droplet freezes, it absorbs water vapor from the air around it. At least 100,000 water droplets are needed to make a single snowflake!

As it gets colder, the snowflake in progress begins to take shape in the form of ice crystals. When molecules form crystals, they like to line up in a nice, orderly fashion. The molecules are almost like building blocks that stack up to form a crystal. Water molecules like to form six-sided ones, which are called hexagonal crystals. Just because snowflakes are hexagonal doesn't mean they all look like stars. Some snowflakes are long and skinny, like needles or columns. Others are flat, like plates, and some branch out to make star shapes.

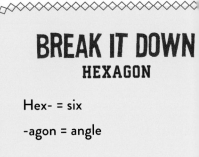

BREAK IT DOWN
HEXAGON

Hex- = six

-agon = angle

Once snowflakes have started to form, things get really interesting. Different factors—like temperature, humidity, and altitude—can all impact the snowflake's shape. The most important factor that causes each snowflake to be unique is the path it takes through the clouds. Since no two snowflakes have the exact same path, no two snowflakes look exactly alike!

SNOWFLAKE SHAPES

Scientists categorize snowflakes into thirty-five different shapes. Here are some of our favorites!

- Radiating dendrites
- Bullet rosettes
- Stellar plates
- Needles
- Capped columns

NATURE'S FIRST-CLASS FLIERS

Now that we're flying high, let's get to know some of the incredible creatures that feel just as much at home in the air as they do on the ground. We're talking about the three Bs—birds, bacteria, and…uh…bizarre creatures you'd never expect to take flight!

My three Bs are bagels, bongos, and baseball.

BIRDS

It's a bird…it's a plane…it's Supermaaaaa—nah, it actually *is* a bird, and that's pretty super. It's easy to take birds for granted; from seagulls at the beach to pigeons in the city, they're everywhere! Birds may be commonplace, but they are amazing creatures. Not only are they evolved from dinosaurs; most birds are lean, mean flying machines that are built to defy gravity. (We'll give an honorable mention to some of our favorite flightless birds, like penguins and ostriches. They're awesome too!)

Even among birds, some species soar above the others. Great frigate birds and common swifts aren't just frequent fliers—flying is how they spend huge chunks of time, without any breaks on land.

Great frigate birds are about the size of a chicken, but their wingspan can be about seven feet. That's as big as a small kayak or large surfboard! These unusual seabirds don't have waterproof feathers, so they can't land on the waves like seagulls and pelicans. If they did, they'd quickly drown. Instead, they soar through the sky at heights up to 12,000 feet above sea level—that's almost as tall as the Rocky Mountains!

Landing on water? Frigate about it!

Frigate birds are the only birds we know of that deliberately fly into clouds to coast along. How do these birds eat when they spend up to eight weeks flying without a break? They've developed a few tricks. Sometimes they fly low to catch small fish that are jumping out of the ocean to escape from predators underwater. Usually, though, they get their meals in a much grosser way. A frigate bird will frighten and harass another bird in flight until it throws up. Then the frigate bird swoops in to eat the puke!

That might be the most disgusting in-flight meal ever.

Common swifts hold an uncommon world record. They spend the most time in flight of any bird species: up to ten months without a single visit to land! These tiny birds are truly built for long-haul flights. They weigh only one and a half ounces—that's less than a tennis ball—and have a wingspan of sixteen inches. That's impressive for such a small bird! They leave Scandinavia in August for a 6,000-mile journey to Africa. Then they turn around and fly back, arriving in Scandinavia in June and spending the next two months caring for their chicks before undertaking the incredible journey all over again. To eat, the swifts catch bugs while they fly. Scientists suspect they even sleep while flying. They have such short, clumsy legs that it's probably for the best that they spend so much time in the air—otherwise, they'd be an easy catch for predators on land.

I once dressed as a common swift for Halloween. I tripped and lost my candy after every house!

FLOCKTACULAR PACKS

We often hear the word "flock" used to describe a group of birds, but some species have their own unique names. Here's a sampling:

- Murder of crows
- Pandemonium of parrots
- Drumming of woodpeckers
- Peep of chickens
- Flamboyance of flamingos
- Parliament of owls
- Exaltation of larks

BACTERIA

Puffy white clouds, drifting along in a calm blue sky…can't you just picture it, so pure and peaceful? Well, picture this: Those clouds are teeming with bacteria that do everything from traveling high into the troposphere to kicking off rainstorms.

It would be cool to find out that bacteria use itsy-bitsy jet packs or ground-to-cloud slingshots to get up there, but scientists haven't found any evidence of that…yet. Instead, scientists think that when a raindrop lands on earth, it can launch bacteria into the air. But some bacteria might not even need rain to blast off! After all, these critters are so small and light that the slightest air current could lift them from the ground and carry them up, up, and away!

In order for rain to form in clouds, there needs to be ice, and we all know that water freezes and turns to ice at thirty-two degrees Fahrenheit. Incredibly, some bacteria are able to raise the freezing temperature of water, so the water can be above thirty-two degrees Fahrenheit when it starts to freeze. This helps precipitation to form—and can even trigger rainstorms by creating heavy droplets. All this is good news for the bacteria, since a rainstorm can help them travel back to earth. While some bacteria seem to have special sky-survival skills, like the ability to withstand exposure to harsh UV rays from the sun, others wouldn't last too long in the clouds. For them, it's all aboard the Raindrop Express back to earth—before the next warm breeze blows them skyward once more!

Tickets, please.

RAINDROP EXPRESS

BIZARRE BUT TRUE!

We might need to replace the ExPLORERR's windshield wipers with lily pads as we head into this next storm.

Raining Frogs and Fish!

Sure, you've heard the expression "It's raining cats and dogs," but how about "frogs and fish"? For thousands of years, people have reported strange instances of storms that rain fish—and even frogs! Are there special clouds that somehow create fish and frogs instead of rain droplets? Nope. Scientists think that especially strong winds, like the ones in hurricanes, tornadoes, and waterspouts, are responsible for this bizarre phenomenon. A tornadic waterspout that zips over a pond can suck up everything in it like a vacuum cleaner—including frogs! Then, as the storm loses energy, the frogs start to fall like ribbit-ribbit rain.

Interestingly, these weird weather reports seem to contain only one type of creature. It's raining either *all* frogs or *all* fish—not a mixture of both. Scientists have a theory: As the wind dies down, it drops all the creatures of similar weight at the same time. So heavy fish might fall on one town, while smaller frogs could fall on another. Either way, let's hope you have a good umbrella!

Ballooning Spiders!

Some spiders scurry…some of them even jump…and then there are the spiders that *fly*! It turns out the silk that spiders spin isn't just useful for weaving webs. They can also release strands of silk that act like a balloon, catching the wind and lifting them off to adventure!

Once they are airborne, these spiders are at the mercy of the wind that carries them aloft. Sometimes they travel a short distance—and sometimes they manage to cross an entire ocean! It all depends on the wind, and these spiders seem to know that very well. In fact, a spider will lift one of its front legs in the air so that it can gauge the wind speed before takeoff. It's kind of like an arachnid preflight check. These tiny pilots know exactly what they're doing!

Flying Squid!

How in the world can a squid—designed to glide through ocean waters—take to the sky and *fly* distances of almost one hundred feet? They don't even have wings! Well, one species of squid has a secret technique that scientists discovered in 2013. First, the squid sucks in a bunch of seawater—then shoots the water out of its body so forcefully that it becomes airborne!

I'm in the squid zone!

After that, it uses its fins and tentacles like wings to propel itself through the air. When its fast flight comes to an end, the squid tucks its fins and tentacles back in for a smooth dive into the ocean.

As many as twenty squid have taken flight together, just like a flock of birds—but why? Scientists think they might be trying to escape from predators in the ocean.

Road Trip SOUVENIR

"I SURVIVED THE FROG RAIN" T-SHIRT

Check out the souvenir *and* fashion statement of the millennium—the "I Survived the Frog Rain" T-shirt! For the most authentic frog rain experience, you could wander around outside, hoping...and waiting... for a frog shower. Or you could simply visit one of the places that has experienced this weird phenomenon:

- **Kansas City, Missouri, 1873**: A tornado probably carried this frog-storm to Kansas City, since there were no lakes or swamps nearby.

- **Dubuque, Iowa, 1882**: The little frogs that tumbled from the sky had frozen into hail!

- **Calgary, Canada, 1921**: When frogs rained on Calgary, the neighborhood cats chowed down at the unexpected all-you-can-eat frog buffet!

- **Odžaci, Serbia, 2005**: Thousands of tiny frogs rained down on this small town—then started hopping around, looking for water!

UP IN THE AIR

We're taking the ExPLORRER even higher into the earth's atmosphere and waving ta-ta to the animals sharing the clouds with us. What's happening up here may feel far removed from life on the ground, but it's super important and has a huge impact on the entire planet!

Carbon Dioxide: Friend or Foe?

Carbon dioxide is *everywhere*. In fact, you—yes, you!—are making some right now. Every time you exhale, you send a puff of carbon dioxide into the world. It turns out this gas is helpful—but if there's too much of it in the air, it can also be harmful.

Before we get to the good, the bad, and the ugly, we need to take a closer look at the molecule itself. Carbon dioxide is also known as CO_2. That's because each carbon dioxide molecule has one carbon atom and two oxygen atoms. It's a colorless gas with no smell, and on its own, it's not a bad thing. People and animals exhale it, which is good news for plants, since plants need CO_2 to make energy, in a process called photosynthesis. Of course, plants return the favor by creating fresh oxygen for us to breathe.

SUPER COOL SCIENTIST

DR. ANNE CO

Dr. Anne Co is a professor of chemistry at the Ohio State University and an associate fellow at the Center for Automotive Research (C-A-R for short—get it?). Her specialty is electrochemistry, which means she's interested in how to make electricity with a chemical reaction (instead of using things like coal). Anne is really curious about how electrons move, which is useful when thinking about how cars will run in the future. One exciting possibility for powering cars is fuel cells. Fuel cells generate electricity, which can power cars without releasing excess amounts of carbon dioxide into the atmosphere. Between fuel cells and other high-performance batteries being developed, scientists like Anne think that the future of cars will be electrified—which is better for the environment and the atmosphere!

The carbon dioxide in the atmosphere is important, because without it life as we know it wouldn't exist. As the sun shines down on earth, our planet reflects this energy back into the air as heat. Gases like oxygen and nitrogen let that heat pass right back out into space—but not carbon dioxide. Carbon dioxide traps a lot of the heat. It acts like a blanket, keeping the earth nice and cozy. Without some carbon dioxide in the atmosphere, the earth would be an icy, frozen wasteland.

But it turns out that you can have too much of a good thing. When humans invented factories powered by coal and cars powered by gas, we started releasing lots of carbon dioxide into the atmosphere. These fuels are carbon-based, so they release carbon dioxide when we burn them. As we've built more factories and power plants and cars, we've put more and more CO_2 into the atmosphere.

And not only are we increasing the amount of CO_2—we're decreasing the number of plants around us by chopping down forests and building cities. As we mentioned, plants take in carbon dioxide, removing it from in the air. Some of our biggest trees, like the ones in tropical rain forests, are getting chopped down at an alarming rate. Without those giant forests taking up the CO_2, we are left with a lot more of it in the atmosphere.

So what was once a nice cozy blanket of CO_2 has gotten thicker and thicker, trapping more and more heat. And now things are warming up—fast.

The increase of CO_2 is leading to changes in our climate. Even small increases in temperature can lead to big problems, like melting ice caps, rising sea levels, and more severe weather.

But reducing the amount of carbon dioxide we put into the atmosphere will help fight this change. All over the world, scientists and inventors are working on new technologies so that we can reduce our carbon dioxide output.

FACT-ASTIC VOYAGE

It's easy to confuse weather and climate. Here's the difference: Weather is what happens on a daily basis, like sun, rain, wind, or snow. Climate describes the weather we experience over a longer period of time in a specific place.

UPPER ATMOSPHERE

Time to wave goodbye to the troposphere and see what's happening in the upper ranges of our atmosphere—and beyond!

Now Entering the Ozone

Ozone is a pale blue gas with a sweet, sharp smell.

Sometimes you can smell it (or feel it tingle your nostrils) just before a thunderstorm, because bolts of lightning can produce it. Ozone is highly explosive *and* poisonous. It's naturally occurring and can also be the product of pollution from power plants and cars. Too much ozone down at the earth's surface can cause coughing, chest pain, and irritated eyes.

But just like carbon dioxide, having ozone in our atmosphere is important to our survival. Let's learn more by visiting the ozone layer.

The ozone layer is in the stratosphere, just beyond the troposphere. It's made up of ozone molecules, which are three oxygen atoms bonded together (also known as O_3). In the stratosphere, ozone molecules don't cause any problems for humans like they would if they were much lower, in the troposphere (where we breathe). Instead, they do us a big favor by absorbing some of the dangerous radiation from the sun.

The ozone blocks harmful rays. To them it's more like the Oh-No-Zone!

Without the ozone layer, life on earth would be infinitely more dangerous. Harmful radiation would bombard the planet at much higher levels, which could cause people and animals to suffer burns, eye damage, and even cancers.

The ozone layer naturally changes shape and thickness throughout the year, but in the early 1970s, scientists started to notice that it was changing at an alarming rate. They called it a hole in the ozone, but in reality it was more like a patchy layer in the stratosphere that had far fewer ozone molecules than expected.

It turns out humans were making chemicals like chlorofluorocarbons (clor-oh-floor-oh-car-bons—phew, no wonder that word was abbreviated to CFCs) that basically eat ozone molecules. Scientists knew we had to act fast to stop the ozone layer from getting even patchier. As a result, many chemicals that damage ozone molecules, like CFCs, have been banned, and the whole world now knows how important it is to protect the ozone layer. After all, our health depends on it.

Dancing Sky Delights!

The earth is full of many jaw-dropping sights, but perhaps the jaw-dropping-est of all are the auroras. Auroras—also called the northern lights or southern lights—appear at night, usually near the North and South Poles. Picture waves of green, yellow, and purple light streaking high above you—like some kind of sky-sized lava lamp!

So what's behind these epic light shows? It all starts with the sun. The sun doesn't just give off light; it also spits out a stream of charged particles called solar wind. Solar wind may sound like a nice, relaxing space breeze, but in reality it is super hot, super dangerous stuff! If it hit the earth, we'd be in trouble. Luckily, we have an amazing magnetic field (learn more on page 8) acting like a shield to protect us. That magnetic field redirects the solar wind so it flows around the earth instead of crashing into it. But some of the solar wind manages to sneak into our atmosphere near the north and south poles.

That solar wind is full of energy, and when it hits the gases in our atmosphere, those gases get super excited. It's sort of like when you eat six bowls of sugar-frosted choco flakes. You get really bouncy for a bit, but then your energy levels usually crash. The same thing happens to these gases when they are hit with solar wind. First they absorb the energy, but soon after, it leaves them. And how does it leave them? As light! When they give off the energy, it creates beautiful, bright patterns in the sky. The earth really knows how to put on a good show, right?

If you see these lights up north, they are called the aurora borealis. If you see them down south, they are called the aurora australis. And if you see them indoors, call a doctor! There might be something up with your eyes.

PIT STOP

INTERNATIONAL SPACE STATION

No trip to high above the earth would be complete without visiting the most epic human habitat *EVER*! Seriously, this pit stop is truly out of this world. Of course we're talking about the International Space Station (ISS)! The ISS is a floating laboratory about the size of a football field. Countries all over the world helped build it. It orbits the earth about 250 miles above us. It's big enough for six people to live there and has been home to a rotating group of astronauts since the year 2000.

Life in the space station is very different from life on earth. You float around all the time, you strap yourself to a wall to sleep, and the station travels so fast that it circles the earth once every ninety minutes or so. That means the astronauts see fifteen or sixteen sunrises and sunsets every day!

But it's more than just a fun place to float. The ISS is a laboratory, after all. The astronauts on board do important research so we can learn about space and how living there impacts humans. The ISS is just one part of a big plan to eventually send people to Mars and beyond!

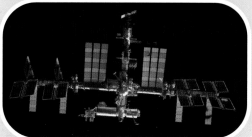

MEGA MATCHUP

LIGHTNING BOLTS VS. SPACE ROCKS

Get ready for an out-of-this-world battle between two dangerous phenomena in the sky: lightning bolts and space rocks! In one corner, lightning bolts! Contrary to popular belief, lightning *can* strike twice in the same place—with all the power of 300 million volts of electricity! And in the other corner, space rocks! We're talking flying rocks from *space* that enter the atmosphere so fast they catch fire! Which one will win in a blaze of glory?

TEAM LIGHTNING BOLT

- Lightning is *hot*—a bolt of lightning can heat the air to more than 50,000 degrees Fahrenheit!

- A blindingly bright bolt of lightning isn't just a shock to the eyes. It's responsible for the rumble of thunder that accompanies it. The gas molecules that make up lightning heat up so quickly that they cause an explosion—and that's what makes thunder *boom*!

- It's no secret that lightning can be deadly. Every year, thousands of people die from being struck by lightning. (The good news is that 90 percent of people who are struck by lightning survive—but if a thunderstorm is approaching, you should always seek shelter right away!)

- About 100 lightning bolts strike the earth every *second*—that adds up to more than 3 billion bolts of lightning a year!

TEAM SPACE ROCK

- Meteorites are space rocks that have taken a wild journey—first as meteoroids that orbit the sun, then as meteors if they happen to enter the earth's atmosphere, and finally as meteorites if they make it to a crash landing on the earth's surface.

- A massive meteorite was responsible for an extinction event 66 million years ago that killed 75 percent of the planet's inhabitants, including the ancient dinosaurs.

- Prepare for impact! More than 6,000 meteorites hit the earth every year—that's about 17 per day!

- Meteorites can be as tiny as a speck of dust or bigger than a giraffe!

- Meteoroids enter the earth's atmosphere at astonishing speeds of up to 160,000 miles per hour, zooming so fast that they burn up. The atmosphere slows down the meteoroid while the flames consume it, making it smaller.

Which dangerous phenomenon is cooler: Lightning Bolts or Space Rocks?

YOUR VERDICT

GET AWAY FROM IT ALL (LITERALLY) ON THE FAR SIDE OF THE MOON!

Hi, Friend!

Wow—we made it all the way to the far side of the moon! It's not what you'd expect from seeing the near side of the moon. Since the moon is tidally locked, only one side of it faces the earth. That means the far side is the one we <u>don't</u> get to see every night. Scientists think the far side of the moon has a thicker crust, resulting in fewer volcanic eruptions, which means there's less lava to fill in craters on that side. So it's pretty rugged looking.

From deep inside the earth, to the oceans, to the land, to the sky, to the atmosphere—we've traveled far, seen a lot, and discovered way more than we dreamed we would. It's always a little sad when an epic trip comes to an end, but at least we have this book to remember it by!

We can't wait to go home!

High (in the sky) fives,

Molly, Marc, and Sanden

Lunar Enthusiast

On Land or Sea

Earth, 238,900 Miles from
    the Moon

HOME, SWEET HOME

Well, we didn't expect to visit the moon, but honestly, it's a perfect end to the trip. Because there's no better way to take in our entire planet than from this distant spot. Several NASA astronauts agree! In 1968, astronauts on NASA's *Apollo 8* mission were sent zooming around the moon. They had a camera with them to document the trip. There's one photo in particular, called *Earthrise*, that has become iconic.

The picture was taken as the crew swung out from behind the back side of the moon. They saw our precious little planet, like a tiny marble, rising above the vast, empty lunar landscape. In the photo, Earth almost seems to glow—in vivid swirls of blue and brown and white. Our oceans. Our lands. Our atmosphere.

It's almost too beautiful for words.

The *Earthrise* photo was soon printed in newspapers around the world. People were *stunned*. They'd never seen the planet this way. Surrounded by cold, dark, empty space, there it was—this one world, so perfectly suited to meet all our needs.

We share it.

We love it.

We protect it—for ourselves and for every creature that lives on this glorious, strange, mysterious planet.

After all, it's home.

ACKNOWLEDGMENTS

This road trip would have never left the garage if it weren't for all our wonderful friends and families. You are the air in our tires, the wipers of our windshields, and the belts in our seats.

Handing a podcast episode to Menaka Wilhelm is like putting the ExPLORERR into cruise control. Totally a smooooooth ride. Rosie duPont can always fill our tanks with her amazing vocal gymnastics. Kristina Lopez is a digital queen and knows how to jazz up a roadside attraction.

Monster truck–sized thank-yous go out to Alex Schaffert, Lily Kim, Phyllis Fletcher, Jon Sklaroff, Tsering Yangcheng, Kris Cramer, Angie Enger, Jennifer Lai, David Zha, Ruby Guthrie, Ava Kian, Kunsang Dorjee, Steve Griffith, Veronica Rodriguez, Cameron Wiley, Johnny Vince Evans, Rob Byers, Corey Schreppel, Eric Romani, Anna Weggel, Eric Ringham, Sam Choo, John Miller, Rachel Dennis, Lauren Dee, and Jon Lambert.

Sam Gentry is our map—without her, we would be lost. Patience and persistence are just two of the Ps she's known for. Albert Lee is a mayor, waiting to hand over a key to the city when you arrive. Mega shout-outs to Megan Bryant, whose words were like a freshly paved road. Anybody who gets captured by the ink of Serge Seidlitz should consider themselves lucky. Thanks to everyone at Little, Brown Books for Young Readers: Megan Tingley, Jackie Engel, Lisa Yoskowitz, David Caplan, Karina Granda, Neil Swaab, Jen Graham, Siena Koncsol, Stefanie Hoffman, Savannah Kennelly, Victoria Stapleton, and Christie Michel.

Big, huge, special thanks to every kid who has been a cohost; sent us mystery sounds, drawings, and questions; read our books; come to a live event; or has just looked out at the world and wondered. This book is for you! We are forever indebted to the scientists who share their work and passion with us and help us understand this amazing planet.

From Sanden: To Kathy, my fiercest advocate, my cherished adviser, my best friend. Hugs and kisses to Felix, welcome to the world, pal! Cuddles and scritches to Penelope A. Poodle. A hearty high five to my family for the endless support. And to my friends, of all the wonders in the world, your friendship is by far the most amazing. Thank you.

From Molly: The biggest thanks imaginable to my family, who love me so fiercely, support me so completely, and keep me well stocked with snacks on every journey. And to my friends, who cheer me on in all the ways, give me directions when I get lost, and also bring me snacks. One million hugs to Andy and Lulu for being the best road trip companions on the entire planet.

From Marc: To the world's best navigator, Vikki Krekler. To Coco Sanchez—I can't wait to see the road trips you take! To Skip and Jody for always being there, even when I didn't notice. To Ella for all her fluffy goodness.

LISTEN ON WITH

To dive deeper and learn more about our astonishing planet, journey over to brainson.org and check out these episodes from our podcast!

Can you dig to the center of the earth?
April 21, 2020

Smash: When continents collide!
November 21, 2017

How do volcanoes erupt?
February 22, 2015

What's behind the waves and tides?
August 30, 2016

What's in your water?
May 1, 2018

Why is the ocean salty?
March 14, 2017

The wonderful weirdness of water
May 22, 2018

Burning rivers of fire
August 7, 2018

Going underground at Wind Cave National Park
December 26, 2016

SELECTED BIBLIOGRAPHY

 PART I: INTO THE EARTH

"Animals and Earthquake Prediction." US Geological Survey. Accessed June 2020. https://www.usgs.gov/natural-hazards/earthquake-hazards/science/animals-earthquake-prediction?qt-science_center_objects=0#qt-science_center_objects

Ault, Alicia. "Ask Smithsonian: What's the Deepest Hole Ever Dug?" *Smithsonian Magazine*, February 19, 2015. https://www.smithsonianmag.com/smithsonian-institution/ask-smithsonian-whats-deepest-hole-ever-dug-180954349

Blackman, Donna. "Can you dig to the center of the Earth?" Interview by *Brains On!*, American Public Media, April 21, 2020. https://www.brainson.org/episode/2020/04/21/can-you-dig-to-the-center-of-the-earth

King, Hobart M. "Interesting Facts and Information about Diamonds." *Geology and Earth Science News and Information*. Accessed June 2020. https://geology.com/articles/diamond-information

"Mountains." *National Geographic*. Accessed June 2020. https://www.nationalgeographic.com/science/earth/surface-of-the-earth/mountains

Parcheta, Carolyn. "How do volcanoes erupt?" Interview by *Brains On!*, American Public Media, October 2, 2017. https://www.brainson.org/episode/2015/02/22/how-do-volcanoes-erupt

Scharer, Kate. "Smash: When continents collide!" Interview by *Brains On!*, American Public Media, November 21, 2017. https://www.brainson.org/episode/2017/11/21/smash-when-continents-collide

Tikoo, Sonia. "Finding your way without a map." Interview by *Brains On!*, American Public Media, November 20, 2018. https://www.brainson.org/episode/2018/11/20/cardinal-directions-compass

Tyrrell, Kelly April. "Oldest fossils ever found show life on Earth began before 3.5 billion years ago." *University of Wisconsin–Madison News*, December 18, 2017. https://news.wisc.edu/oldest-fossils-found-show-life-began-before-3-5-billion-years-ago

"Zircon Chronology: Dating the Oldest Material on Earth." American Museum of Natural History. Accessed June 2020. https://www.amnh.org/learn-teach/curriculum-collections/earth-inside-and-out/zircon-chronology-dating-the-oldest-material-on-earth

PART 2: WET, WILD, AND WEIRD

Andrei, Mihai. "Why some creatures in the deep sea grow to enormous sizes." *ZME Science*, June 7, 2019. https://www.zmescience.com/science/biology/deep-sea-giant-creature

Ashworth, Jr., William B. "Scientist of the Day: Frederick Otis Barton, Jr." Linda Hall Library, June 5, 2019. https://www.lindahall.org/frederick-otis-barton-jr

Carilli, Jessica. "What's behind the waves and tides?" Interview by *Brains On!*, American Public Media, August 30, 2016. https://www.brainson.org/episode/2016/08/30/whats-behind-the-waves-and-tides

"The Cuyahoga River." National Park Service, May 20, 2020. https://www.nps.gov/cuva/learn/kidsyouth/the-cuyahoga-river.htm

Edwards, Mark. "What's in your water?" Interview by *Brains On!*, American Public Media, May 1, 2018. https://www.brainson.org/episode/2018/05/01/whats-in-your-water

Gould, Jim, and Carol Graves-Gould. "Deep Sea vs. Outer Space." Interview by *Brains On!*, American Public Media, July 18, 2017. https://www.brainson.org/episode /2017/07/18/deep-sea-vs-outer-space

Hurst, Harold Edwin. "Nile River." *Britannica*, November 7, 2019. https://www.britannica .com/place/Nile-River

"Hydrothermal Vent Life." Woods Hole Oceanographic Institution. Accessed May 2020. https://divediscover.whoi.edu/hydrothermal-vents/vent-life-2

Jha, Alok. "The wonderful weirdness of water." Interview by *Brains On!*, American Public Media, May 22, 2018. https://www.brainson.org/episode/2018/05/22/weirdwater

Kraynick, George. "Water, water everywhere—but how does it get there?" Interview by *Brains On!*, American Public Media, July 8, 2014. https://www.brainson.org/episode /2014/07/08/water-water-everywhere-but-how-does-it-get-there

"Lake." *National Geographic.* Accessed May 2020. https://www.nationalgeographic.org /encyclopedia/lake

Lam, Phoebe. "Why is the ocean salty?" Interview by *Brains On!*, American Public Media, March 14, 2017. https://www.brainson.org/episode/2017/03/14/why-is -the-ocean-salty

"Largest Eye in the World, Giant Squid." Smithsonian Institution. Accessed May 2020. https://ocean.si.edu/ocean-life/invertebrates/largest-eye-world-giant-squid

Linder, Douglas O. "Simply Superior: The Greatest Lake." Lake Superior, 2014. http:// law2.umkc.edu/faculty/projects/ftrials/superior/superior.html

"MUSA: Museo Subacuatico de Arte." MUSA Isla Mujeres. Accessed May 2020. http:// musaislamujeres.com/#aboutmusa

"Ocean Trenches." Woods Hole Oceanographic Institution. Accessed May 2020. https://www.whoi.edu/know-your-ocean/ocean-topics/seafloor-below/ocean-trenches

"Ocean Zones." *NatureWorks*. Accessed May 2020. https://nhpbs.org/natureworks/nwep6c.htm

"Remotely operated vehicles." Monterey Bay Aquarium Research Institute. Accessed May 2020. https://www.mbari.org/at-sea/vehicles/remotely-operated-vehicles

"River." *National Geographic*. Accessed May 2020. https://www.nationalgeographic.org/encyclopedia/river

"Rivers, Streams, and Creeks." US Geological Survey. Accessed May 2020. https://www.usgs.gov/special-topic/water-science-school/science/rivers-streams-and-creeks?qt-science_center_objects=0#qt-science_center_objects

Samsel, Frank. "Burning rivers of fire." Interview by *Brains On!*, American Public Media, August 7, 2018. https://www.brainson.org/episode/2018/08/07/cuyahoga-river-fire

Sandrick, Bob. "Q & A: Frank Samsel." *FreshWater Cleveland*, May 11, 2017. https://www.freshwatercleveland.com/features/FrankSamsel051117.aspx

Spector, Dina. "What Sand Grains Look Like Through A Microscope." *Business Insider*, January 27, 2014. https://www.businessinsider.com/images-of-sand-grains-through-a-microscope-2014-1

"What are El Niño and La Niña?" National Ocean Service, National Oceanic and Atmospheric Administration, February 10, 2020. https://oceanservice.noaa.gov/facts/ninonina.html

"What Is the Gulf Stream?" SciJinks, National Oceanic and Atmospheric Administration, October 8, 2020. https://scijinks.gov/gulf-stream

 # PART 3: TOTALLY GROUNDED

Bunch, Fred. "Making the sands sing at Great Sand Dunes National Park." Interview by *Brains On!*, American Public Media, December 28, 2016. https://www.brainson.org/episode/2016/12/28/making-the-sands-sing-at-great-sand-dunes-national-park

"Canyon." *National Geographic*. Accessed July 2020. https://www.nationalgeographic.org/encyclopedia/canyon

"The Desert Biome." UC Museum of Paleontology, University of California–Berkeley. Accessed July 2020. https://ucmp.berkeley.edu/exhibits/biomes/deserts.php

"Grand Canyon: Wildlife." National Park Service, January 20, 2017. https://www.nps.gov/grca/learn/nature/wildlife.htm

"How does sand form?" National Ocean Service, National Oceanic and Atmospheric Administration, April 9, 2020. https://oceanservice.noaa.gov/facts/sand.html#

"Ice, Snow, and Glaciers and the Water Cycle." US Geological Survey. Accessed July 2020. https://www.usgs.gov/special-topic/water-science-school/science/ice-snow-and-glaciers-and-water-cycle

Krulwich, Robert. "Which Is Greater, the Number of Sand Grains on Earth or Stars in the Sky?" *National Public Radio*, September 17, 2012. https://www.npr.org/sections/krulwich/2012/09/17/161096233/which-is-greater-the-number-of-sand-grains-on-earth-or-stars-in-the-sky#

Machaca, Patricia. "Soil: Can you dig it?" Interview by *Brains On!*, American Public Media, December 18, 2018. https://www.brainson.org/episode/2014/08/12/soil-can-you-dig-it

Ohms, Mark. "Going underground at Wind Cave National Park." Interview by *Brains On!*, American Public Media, July 2, 2019. https://www.brainson.org/episode/2016/12/26/going-underground-at-wind-cave-national-park

"Sand Dunes: How Sand Dunes Are Formed." DesertUSA. Accessed July 2020. https://www.desertusa.com/geofacts/sanddune.html

Siminski, Peter. "The Desert Adaptations of Birds and Mammals." Arizona-Sonora Desert Museum. Accessed July 2020. https://www.desertmuseum.org/books/nhsd_adaptations_birds.php

Smith, Jeremy M. B. "Desert." *Britannica*, March 13, 2020. https://www.britannica.com/science/desert

Tikoo, Sonia. "Finding your way without a map." Interview by *Brains On!*, American Public Media, November 20, 2018. https://www.brainson.org/episode/2018/11/20/cardinal-directions-compass

"Why Should We Study Rocks?" Rock Around the World, Arizona State University. Accessed July 2020. http://ratw.asu.edu/aboutrocks_why.html

PART 4: SKY'S THE LIMIT

"Basic Ozone Layer Science." US Environmental Protection Agency, September 24, 2018. https://www.epa.gov/ozone-layer-protection/basic-ozone-layer-science

Blumenfeld, Kenny. "Thunder, lightning and tornadoes: Where do they come from?" Interview by *Brains On!*, American Public Media, September 4, 2017. https://www.brainson.org/episode/2015/08/13/thunder-lightning-and-tornadoes-where-do-they-come-from

"Can it rain frogs, fish, and other objects?" Library of Congress. Accessed August 2020. https://www.loc.gov/everyday-mysteries/item/can-it-rain-frogs-fish-and-other -objects

Co, Anne. "The future of fuel, and the problem with exhaust (Road Trip pt. 2)." Interview by *Brains On!*, American Public Media, June 16, 2017. https://www.brainson.org /episode/2017/06/16/the-future-of-fuel-and-the-problem-of-exhaust-road-trip -pt-2

Coleman, Fritz. "How do meteorologists predict the weather?" Interview by *Brains On!*, American Public Media, November 25, 2015. https://www.brainson.org/episode /2015/11/25/how-do-meteorologists-predict-the-weather

"The Far Side of the Moon—And All the Way Around." NASA, March 11, 2011. https:// www.nasa.gov/mission_pages/LRO/news/lro-farside.html

Fessenden, Marissa. "Snowflakes All Fall in One of 35 Different Shapes." *Smithsonian Magazine*, December 30, 2014. https://www.smithsonianmag.com/smart-news /snowflakes-all-fall-one-35-different-shapes-180953760

Franz, Julia. "Bacteria are thriving in the sky—and they influence the weather." *The World*, March 22, 2017. https://www.pri.org/stories/2017-03-22/bacteria-are-thriving -sky-and-they-influence-weather

Johnson, Aleisha. "My air came from where?! How oxygen gets around." Interview by *Brains On!*, American Public Media, February 26, 2019. https://www.brainson.org /episode/2019/02/26/my-air-came-from-where-how-oxygen-gets-around

Libbrecht, Ken. "Why are no two snowflakes the same?" Interview by *Brains On!*, American Public Media, January 13, 2016. https://www.brainson.org/episode/2016/01/13 /why-are-no-two-snowflakes-the-same

"Living Large with the International Space Station." *Brains On!*, American Public Media, February 21, 2016. https://www.brainson.org/episode/2016/02/21/living -large-with-the-international-space-station

"Meteors & Meteorites." NASA Science Solar System Exploration, December 19, 2019. https://solarsystem.nasa.gov/asteroids-comets-and-meteors/meteors-and-meteorites /in-depth

Moran, Joe. "Earthrise: The story behind our planet's most famous photo." *The Guardian*, December 22, 2018. https://www.theguardian.com/artanddesign/2018/dec/22 /behold-blue-plant-photograph-earthrise

"Severe Weather 101: Frequently Asked Questions About Lightning." National Severe Storms Laboratory. Accessed August 2020. https://www.nssl.noaa.gov/education /svrwx101/lightning/faq

"10 interesting things about air." NASA, September 12, 2016. https://climate.nasa.gov /news/2491/10-interesting-things-about-air

"Waterspouts." Ocean Today, National Oceanic and Atmospheric Administration. Accessed August 2020. https://oceantoday.noaa.gov/waterspouts

"Weather Fronts." UCAR Center for Science Education. Accessed August 2020. https:// scied.ucar.edu/learning-zone/how-weather-works/weather-fronts

"Weather Watching: The birth of forecasts." *Brains On!*, American Public Media, March 3, 2020. https://www.brainson.org/episode/2020/03/03/weather-watching-the-birth -of-forecasts

"What Is the International Space Station?" NASA Knows!, November 30, 2011. https:// www.nasa.gov/audience/forstudents/k-4/stories/nasa-knows/what-is-the-iss-k4.html

"What's the Difference Between Weather and Climate?" National Centers for Environmental Information, National Oceanic and Atmospheric Administration, August 7, 2020. https://www.ncei.noaa.gov/news/weather-vs-climate

INDEX

ABOUT THE AUTHORS

MOLLY BLOOM, MARC SANCHEZ, and **SANDEN TOTTEN** are the creators of American Public Media's *Brains On!* and the authors of *It's Alive* and *Earth Friend Forever*. They are real-life best buds who spend a lot of time trying to make one another laugh with puns, fart jokes, and funny voices. Molly likes to sing and eat noodles with cottage cheese and loves the kind of weather where you can wear a sweater and sandals at the same time. Marc likes running and eating tacos and hopes to one day reconnect with his childhood imaginary friend, Pocho. Sanden likes arranging flowers and eating vegan pizza and wants to start a punk band with his poodle, Penelope. They invite you to visit them at brainson.org or @Brains_On.